T0193460

God
IS A VERB!
Selah

LYNN KELLER

authorHOUSE®

AuthorHouse™
1663 Liberty Drive
Bloomington, IN 47403
www.authorhouse.com
Phone: 1 (800) 839-8640

NIV
THE HOLY BIBLE, NEW INTERNATIONAL VERSION®, NIV® Copyright © 1973,
1978, 1984, 2011 by Biblica, Inc.™ Used by permission. All rights reserved worldwide.

Published by AuthorHouse 02/13/2019

ISBN: 978-1-7283-0000-9 (sc)
ISBN: 978-1-5462-7999-0 (e)

Library of Congress Control Number: 2019901636

Print information available on the last page.

Any people depicted in stock imagery provided by Getty Images are models,
and such images are being used for illustrative purposes only.
Certain stock imagery © Getty Images.

This book is printed on acid-free paper.

Contents

Orientation

This book began in my first class at Cornell University. We were asked whether the purpose of religion was to believe in Jesus or be nice to others. I was the sole student who chose the golden rule. Probably, the results would be different these many years later. It was shocking to me since not everyone was even a Christian. Even then, there should have been a debate.

Did others think this was a right or wrong question? Was this about getting a good grade rather than getting an education?

Later in the lecture, our instructor told us that at Cornell, we would learn *how* to think, rather than *what* to think.

That class not only set the tone for me at Cornell but also for the rest of my life, particularly with regard to God, religion, and philosophy.

For me, Buckminster Fuller said it best: "Faith is much better than belief. Belief is when someone else does the thinking."

In these decades, I have found it particularly bizarre to have been told what I think or believe—*often*. As a rule, when this happens, it is about what the other person believes, not what I believe, think, or care about.

This book is my journey since that day. I am continuing with my values and concepts always at the core. I always pay attention to the patterns, so perhaps my journey will support yours. I consider the two trees in the garden of Eden to be an organizing system, not a belief system.

When I was four, I could not remember which came first, six or seven, because they both began with an "s." I was telling my father that I should only be expected to count one past my birthday. My father said, "Ross is only two, and he can count to ten. I am thirty-two, and I can count past one hundred." Just then, I looked over his shoulder and saw the clock! Aha! I had a cheat sheet. Numbers had a place and an order. Tens went in a line, and twelves went in a circle. Numbers had relationships and patterns.

Later that day, I surprised my mother to no end. I was doing well with math, so she asked, "What is six times eight?"

Almost instantly, I responded, "Forty-eight." My life changed just that fast.

The tree of knowledge from Genesis is just as simple. Know which way you are going, and organize your thoughts accordingly. It is a framework for organizing concepts. Any data can be put into the system. It is a relationship model that enables a person to evaluate and organize data. The framework is not sacred. It can be used for sacred or secular information. It works well for science and technology.

Having an organizing system and basic universal concepts will enable a respectful and comprehensible dialogue from both similar and dissimilar stances on morals, philosophy, and religion.

This work is dedicated to the ability to look at things that are seemingly different and find the similarities. Likewise, one can see the differences and find common ground.

My friend, now deceased, identified himself as a "compassionate atheist." He lived this "Way of Return" without ever getting waylaid by beliefs. Would you discuss your faith with him? The Way of Return is dedicated to the ability to discuss your faith with him.

My first class was called "Orientation." That is the foundation for this small book.

Prologue

GOD IS A VERB

God is a verb, a dynamic, creative action,
Not the abstraction,
But rather,
The doing and the being,
The kind and the caring.
The profound and the personal
Expansive, yet intimate,
Orderly yet free

God is the joy and brilliance of happening
The movement of the known and unknown
The mystery and the truth
Yes, God is a verb in constant action and love.

God is the mastering of chaos, of static states,
Of disorder and disharmony
Into a vast meaningful peace and harmony.

1

CONCEPT

A rose has a front.
A rose has a back.

God has neither a front nor a back.

God does not have corporality.
He has no body. He has no limits.

Roses have substance. God does not.

Rather than thinking about God as a form with the
characteristics and qualities of physical presence, we
shift to actions, movement, and attributes of
happening and being.

Once we realize God is not a noun, we come to realize God is action.
God creates.
God is a verb.

2

GOD IS A VERB

When asked to describe Himself, God said, "יהוה," which is vocalized as "Yud He Vauv He." This is regularly translated as "I Am that I Am." More properly, the translation is "I Shall Be as I Shall Be." What a difference a verb makes! The tense of the verb is all telling and all meaning.

Present tense is literally an *is*. This tense does not indicate anything other than a current presence. It clearly refers to a noun. The concept of change does not exist as a noun without time. The term *shall be* creates a paradigm shift for the concept of God. By God stating Himself in a future tense, He is creating a different reality. God is a changing dynamic. God becomes *doing* rather than an *it*. God is action and not form. God is a verb.

"I Shall Be as I Shall Be" indicates a future tense. God is changing and becoming as the process of creating. Past and present tenses would have meant a God already formed—a noun. Considering God as a verb requires thinking about every single aspect concerning God in a new context.

Hebrew is read from right to left. Notice there is an opening on the far left in the left side of the letter *He* or *Het*. This means that people can choose to leave, but there is always the opening to return.

Rather than thinking about God as a form with the characteristics and qualities of physical presence, we shift to actions and attributes of happening and being. We begin thinking about wind and light and temperature and time. We suddenly look at God the Creator as a manifesting entity or action rather than as a big magician in the sky. Imagine the force that creates everything from the very smallest triangle as a neutron to the most complex of physical beings and the cosmos. The concept of the *force* is akin to the *creation* as a state of being.

God as an action is creation.

> And Moses said unto G-d: "Behold, when I come unto the children of Israel, and shall say unto them: The G-d of your fathers hath sent me unto you; and they shall say to me: What is His name? what shall I say unto them?"
> And G-d said unto Moses: "I AM THAT I AM"; and He said: "Thus shalt thou say unto the children of Israel: I AM hath sent me unto you." (Exodus 3:13–14)

God Is a Verb and our next book, *The Way of Return*, are not Kabbalah. However, there are concepts that are valid for this book since both are concerned with our relationship with God and with the two trees in the garden of Eden.

Beyond the paradigm of the tree is the "Ein Sof," which are aspects of God that are beyond our capacity to comprehend. Ein Sof means "without end." Nouns as a concept generally have form and limits.

One of the seventy-two names of God is Bal Tachlis, which means "God is not bound or limited in any way." As a verb, God is the action in the heavens rather than a being, a noun, in the sky. God does not have a beginning or an end, both of which would be considered boundaries. Any form of the physical would be bounded. God is not bounded by time or place.

Furthermore, the challenge for us is to discover God's relationship to us as human beings on planet Earth rather than to attempt to understand God other than in a variety of aspects. He is totally beyond human. Thus, we concentrate on attributes of God that are comprehensible.

The very concept of God as a verb shifts the focus into relationship rather than form and the limitations of boundaries.

The attributes of God shift in language. Adjectives that apply to God do not apply to verbs. Words describing God and God's characteristics just do not apply to rules of grammar. God is compassionate. However, compassion is a noun. Compassion implies doing. That is a limitation of language, not of God.

The problem is that nomenclature relates to human concepts and labels as verbs, adverbs, adjectives, and nouns, which skews (distorts) the communication. We are left with terminology to describe the inexplicable with terms that limit and alter the intention. The words used herein are aimed at the context of the statements "A rose is a noun. God is a verb."

Attributes are used as defining actions and characteristics of God, who is an action. He is a state of being and awareness without physicality. The inadequacies of our languages are an indication of our inability to conceive of God as a consciousness.

We are taught that God has many dimensions, of which we can only identify and approximate a few. Some dimensions and characteristics are comprehensible in the abstract but not achievable. Certainly most aspects of God are far beyond our human experience and comprehension.

The challenge for us is to bring all our comprehension, actions, and reactions into the most basic levels. The more clarity we have in the most elementary concepts, the more aligned we can be to our purpose for being and our life on this planet.

Since God is not a noun, consider this truth: God does not have a form in any criteria. Since God is not a noun, God cannot and does not have a gender. Most animals have gender and come in pairs. God creates pairs, but God is never other than One. The pronouns *he* and *she* are gender specific. The reason God is referred to as "He" is not that He is male but because there are no pronouns that are applicable. Consequently, the capitalized *He* refers to God.

There was a great children's program called *Schoolhouse Rock* to teach kids with song. There were two wonderful songs to explain classifications of words as parts of speech. "A Noun Is a Person, Place, or Thing," written by Lynn Ahrens, clearly stated that which we all know. In fact, we use the word *thing* in place of a name with astonishing regularity.

However, *no one* calls God "a thing" or "my thing." The song by Bob Dorough titled "Verb: That's What's Happening," could actually be about God. Following are two appropriate stanzas.

I get my thing in action (Verb!)
In being (Verb!)
In doing (Verb!)
In saying
A verb expresses action, being, or state of being
A verb makes a statement
Yeah, a verb tells it like it is!
(Verb! That's what's happening)
I get my thing in action
(Verb, that's what's happening)
To work (Verb!)
To play (Verb!)
To live (Verb!)
To love (Verb!

Deeds are verbs—only verbs. Acts of kindness are verbs and not nouns. Creation is a noun that implies a verb.

Then it occurred to me that God is all the happy, creative, positive verbs. All the negative verbs are not connected or manifesting God. They do reflect our egos, and our egos can manifest either positive or negative actions.

Transcend is an intransitive verb. It applies very well to God as a verb. It means to rise above or extend notably beyond ordinary limits. It does not have an object. It is an action of going beyond all boundaries in thoughts, concepts, and capabilities. In other words, God is a beingness beyond our human capabilities to even envision or perceive. Perhaps God as performing miracles is the closest context we have.

The definition of the verb *create* is given in *Webster's Dictionary.*

to make or produce (something): to cause (something new) to exist

to cause (a particular situation) to exist

to produce (something new, such as a work of art) by using your talents and imagination

When we consider the attributes of God, none of them are nouns. God is the action. God creates. The limitations are in our languages and in our comprehension.

God said, "I shall be as I shall be." God did. God does. God will do. "Know Me by my deeds." The action continues beyond the infinite.

The boundary that God is always beyond is that of human speech, languages, and classifications.

3

SELAH IN THE TITLE

Stop! Think intently!

The title *God Is a Verb* was the context for this book. Then, suddenly, I found the title was taken. It has an ISBN number.

Oops.

The new title was almost instantaneous: *Selah*. Selah was already a major section of this book. It is found most often in Psalms. I was taught that *selah* means "stop and think about it," and that is my definition. When I read the word *selah*, I instantly stop and think with dedication and intensity. To me, it is an indication of strategic importance. It is an emphasis and a call to be repeated. Did you hear what I said? Do you understand why I said it and what it means? What does it mean to you? How does it fit your context?

Is it the same? Be clear about this before you proceed. Do not forget. Reflect.

It comes most often after the statement or verse. It is akin to a command. Pay attention to this aspect specifically and with the intent to understand.

However, the Aish rabbi gave this explanation:

The Talmud (Eruvin 54a) says that selah means "forever." The Radak (12th century France) saw it as a musical notation for the singers to raise their voices. And Ibn Ezra (12th century Spain) understood it to mean "true and certain."

Finally, Rabbi S. R. Hirsch, in nineteenth-century Germany, explained that typically selah remains "untranslated" because it has no intrinsic meaning. Rather, it is poetic and adds extra emphasis like someone yelling, "Yahoo!" in joyous emotion.

In this book, it is important to consider Psalm 143, which was the frequent plea by this author from teenage years and beyond. Of the seventy-one instances where the word *selah* is found in Psalms, the specific psalm and context is critical. Psalm 143 is the one I think of. This is an imperative.

> Hear my prayer, O Lord, give ear to my supplications: in thy faithfulness answer me, and in thy righteousness.
>
> And enter not into judgment with thy servant: for in thy sight shall no man living be justified.
>
> For the enemy hath persecuted my soul; he hath smitten my life down to the ground; he hath made me to dwell in darkness, as those that have been long dead.
>
> Therefore is my spirit overwhelmed within me; my heart within me is desolate.
>
> I remember the days of old; I meditate on all thy works; I muse on the work of thy hands.
>
> I stretch forth my hands unto thee: my soul thirsteth after thee, as a thirsty land. *Selah.*
>
> Hear me speedily, O Lord: my spirit faileth: hide not thy face from me, lest I be like unto them that go down into the pit.
>
> Cause me to hear thy lovingkindness in the morning; for in thee do I trust: cause me to know the way wherein I should walk; for I lift up my soul unto thee.
>
> Deliver me, O Lord, from mine enemies: I flee unto thee to hide me.

Teach me to do thy will; for thou art my God: thy spirit is good; lead me into the land of uprightness.

Quicken me, O Lord, for thy name's sake: for thy righteousness' sake bring my soul out of trouble.

And of thy mercy cut off mine enemies, and destroy all them that afflict my soul: for I am thy servant.

I have found occasional online usage citing "selah" as "Praise and think calmly about it." That is lovely, really lovely, but it misses the point of emphasis and clarity. It lacks the imperative, the mandate, and even the plea.

It is nicey-nicey, timid, and wishy-washy. When we read or hear "selah," it is a mandate. Could you interject "selah" to praise and think calmly. This definition has no verve. It is a wonderful idea, but it belongs to a different word. It does not connect to the usage in Psalms. Create a different word for this definition.

Verve is a fabulous word. It means great energy and enthusiasm. It fits with *selah* quite well indeed.

According to *Wikipedia*, *selah* means
1. Amen (Hebrew: "so be it") in that it stresses the truth and importance of the preceding passage;
2. this interpretation is consistent with the meaning of the Semitic root ṣ-l-ḥ also reflected in Arabic cognate salih (variously "valid" [in the logical sense of "truth-preserving"], "honest," and "righteous").
3. Alternatively, selah may mean "forever," as it does in some places in the liturgy (notably the second to last blessing of the Amidah).
4. Another interpretation claims that selah comes from the primary Hebrew root word selah (סָלַה), which means "to hang," and by implication to measure (weigh).

This book accepts these viewpoints and definitions of Selah from *Wikipedia*. There was no declared definition in the times of the Psalms. The perfect quality is that it is most applicable to a verb. The clearest term is "valid."

The idea of measuring is interesting since it is a directive to get high-quality data in your assessment. The intention is to consider the aspects carefully, with precision—in other words, to reflect and study with attention to detail.

Selah is actually an exclamation and emphasis. There is a passion about this word and in using it. As cited earlier, Rabbi Hirsch said that it has "no intrinsic meaning." In that case, it is somewhat like "Hallelujah." In our usage, there is a deeper and wider definition to *selah* than has *hallelujah*.

Remember, every single word in Psalms connects back to the Torah. All were written in the context that "Torah is truth." We are taught if you do not understand any statement in the Torah as truth, keep studying it until you understand the truth.

Therefore, selah implies reconsidering and reflecting back to the source, to the Torah, particularly the book of Genesis. As mentioned, there is no declared definition from the times of the Psalms. It was commonly understood. It connects to the realization that every verse in the Torah is explained by the next two verses.

Selah is properly said at the end of a phrase or concept.

Stop and think with verve! This is valid and important.

Reconsider and repeat it
with passion and verve.

God is a verb—consider it, and celebrate with verve.

4

HIS NAME

'Tia but thy name that is mine enemy:
What's Montague? It is not hand nor foot,
Nor arm, nor face, nor any other part.

Juliet:
What's in a name? That which we call a rose
By any other name would smell as sweet.
Romeo and Juliet (II, ii, 1–2)

What is the proper term for God, a verb?

Verbs do not have a pronoun: he, she, or it. Nouns often have gender-specific qualities, but God, a verb, does not have gender. We refer to God as *He*, capitalized, to differentiate from the pronouns. As such, He does not have gender indications unless someone is attempting to make an issue. In common usage, God capitalized does not refer to a male human being. God capitalized refers to the One and Only Supreme Intelligence, not any gods of human manifestation.

We can and certainly shall continue to discuss or indicate "God." We all have a general concept of what each of us means. "He" capitalized is used as the name for similar universal references. While few actually agree on who or what we call "God," we all understand we are talking about the same universal presence. To use "She" as a substitute for "He" is creating miscommunication by instilling gender identity considerations. "He" does not have a gender. The lowercased "he" is absolutely gender specific.

11

The presence and gender aspects of God are indicated twice in the Torah. In the garden of Eden, the sweet feminine voice of God, called the Sheckinah, talked directly to Adam and Eve. At Mount Sinai, when delivering the first two commandments, God spoke in a thunderous voice that was unbearably loud. Readers generally consider this voice as masculine.

Facetiously, since these are the only times of direct interaction with God, we could call Him "The Voice." That term has already been copyrighted globally in many languages for a media enterprise. It specifically has no sacred connotations.

In Hebrew, there are seventy-two names for God. One name, "Yud he vauv he," is too sacred to be uttered. The solution for Jews is to call God "HaShem," which means "the name." HaShem wisely resolves the issue since "the name" supersedes nomenclature and categorization.

While the name, HaShem, resolves the problem for the Jews, who have the same tradition, it is awkward and without meaning for most others. It also is without relevance in and for the tree of knowledge of good and evil.

The common names, therefore, are limited to "God" and "He," regardless of whether someone is thinking about God as a noun or God as a verb.

A rose is a rose.
God is God.

5

IN THE BEGINNING—BET

The God Idea in Jewish Tradition by Rabbi Israel Konowitz was cited by Elie Wiesel: "Anyone willing to deepen their knowledge of the Jewish tradition's concept of God and His role in history should read this book which combines erudition and wisdom."

It is an awe-inspiring book to say the least. The ninety chapter headings in themselves are a knowledge base of subjects about God Himself.

The following quote by Rabbi Konowitz is from Bereshis, or Genesis, as it is called in Greek and English.

Chapter 1 by Rabbi Konowitz is "Who Is God and What Is His Name?" The thirty-seventh concept states,

> The Pentateuch begins with the words (Gen 1:1), "In the beginning (Bereshis in Hebrew) God created ..."
>
> Why was the world created with the letter bet (the first letter of the word Bereshis)?" Why was it not created with alef (which is the first letter of the Hebrew alphabet)? [The reason is that] the letter bet b has two points, one pointing upward and one downward

and to the back of the letter. If one asks the *bet*, "Who created you?" the first point indicates upward, implying, "He who is above created me." "And what is His name?" The second points backward and says, "The Lord Adonai is His name."

This is a critical concept for this book. God began with the letter bet. This letter contains two points, a pair. They are similar and equal. Thus God created with equilibrium and harmony first of all. A pair of points show that God did not create a hierarchy. God created harmoniously and unified. Bet is one letter with two points, unlike alef, which stands alone. Our universe is based on pairs in equilibrium. Without doubt, our planet and our people were created with the same intention and action.

Opposites and hierarchy are of human origin and consideration. God created in pairs that are in balance always.

If God created in harmony, how did God enable the free-will choice of humans to exist? God *retracted* ever so slightly. That space where God does not exist is the location for our free will.

One of the many aspects of this information is that the letter "alef" implies oneness. It is first and alone. It could signify God, who is the ultimate oneness. Beginning creation with the dual points in the letter bet signifies the pattern we observe continually.

One is divided or becomes two, a pair, always a pair. God continually creates in pairs: two separate but aligned aspects.

We must always work to see the pairs work in harmony and balance, not separation and opposition.

Opposition is a human construct. Opposites are inimitable and antagonistic. They are fundamentally pulling in discord and selfness.

Oppositions are alien from God.

There are no aspects of God that are hierarchical. God is.

Genesis 1:1 is translated as "In the beginning God created the heaven and the earth" and "In the beginning of God's creating the heavens and the earth." Both translations begin with action. God created. This is an action. It is not the description of a noun.

In the 1980s, when I was first studying the tree of life as an organizing system, I was introduced to the work of Stan Tenen on the mathematics of the Hebrew alphabet. He had established his extraordinary lifelong study of the first sentence in the Torah, Bereshis 1:1 (also known as Genesis 1:1).

As I studied, I found numerous studies of patterns in the Torah, the first five books of the Bible. This is obvious since this is the foundation of Judaism. The Bible codes also use patterns from the whole of the Torah. The same goes for all studies of the tree of life and of Kabbalah. The books of the Tanach, which contain most of that which Christians call the Old Testament, all reflect back to the Torah as their source. They are all written with the Torah as context.

The salient point is that there have been continual applications of this ancient wisdom and patterns that are beyond the capacity for any human or group of humans to have created. These multidimensional, intelligent patterns are most readily adapted to uses that involve our own self-awareness and relationships with others. These same patterns can be utilized for

My work is dedicated to patterns in Bereshis/Genesis with a focus on the first two covenants, which happened in the Age of Taurus.

6

RATIONALE

Rationale is the fundamental reason or reasons serving to account for something. This book has some basic principles and concepts that I, as the author, use to support the argument that God is a verb. This chapter reflects my reasoning so that my point of view need not be a deterrent but rather a path to communication.

My information is not frivolous. It may not be customary for many people. I hope you will consider whether you are questioning my assertion or my data. I invite a discussion about both, but please know whether it is about God or about my rationale. I look at the discussion as being about pairs of thoughts, not opposites.

Some clarification is needed.

In human consideration, time is measured by observing our planet rotating with respect to the sun. A rotation takes twenty-four lowercased hours from sunrise to sunrise, for example. In our vocabulary, *day* refers to that rotation. That would be a nanosecond in God's calculations.

God's Day is possibly an eon. An eon is considered to be about a billion years. For the sake of comprehension, God is He capitalized. His Day is Day capitalized.

Some sources consider God's Day as a thousand years. Whether God's Day is a thousand, six thousand, one hundred forty-four thousand, a million, or a billion years is impossible to reckon.

God's Day is a very long, indeterminate period. It can be varying lengths of time. It can refer to cycles of different times and purposes. These long periods are also called "the Long Day."

To complicate periods of time further, our solar calendar year consists of 364 days of twenty-four hours, which contain numerous cycles, and the 365th day is the long day. It is one and a quarter days long. Every four years, an extra day, February 29, is added to validate the two cycles. Thus, our calendar has two distinct sets with separate time periods, relatedness, and meaning.

Second, the Torah is referred to regularly in this book. The Torah is the first five books of the Jewish Bible, the Pentateuch. The Tanach is comprised of most books in the Old Testament. Every book was written in the context of Torah. The Tanach affirms and elucidates the Torah. Included in the Tanach are Psalms and Proverbs.

Torah was an oral tradition for thousands of years, but the main characters lived for centuries. Shem, the son of Adam and Eve, lived until the time of Abraham. There were people who recalled with acute memories. My acceptance of that story is based largely on the long and vital life of Sarai bas Asher, granddaughter of Jacob. She lived many hundreds of years and was able to recall crossing the Red Sea when the waters parted. The stories in Genesis were a living oral history, a very accurate oral record.

According to the oral history of the Jews, there were seventy-two rabbis, six from each of the twelve tribes of Israel, who were called to translate the Torah. The miracle was that all seventy-two produced essentially the same document. There are but six letters that are under question.

The Torah is a holy document written in perfection that no human being could have designed.

As a student of Torah, I noticed that each verse was followed by two that explain it. This is evident throughout all five books. This is the pattern I find in all God does. One is followed or divided into a pair, a complementary pair, aimed at equilibrium.

God never creates division into opposites, which always separate from each other. The separation is always directly against balance and truth.

Torah ends with the letter "l" and starts with "b." Thus LAB or LAV, meaning love, is an endless cycle from God containing only truth and love. If you do not understand that it is about love, study it until you do. If you do not understand God has been trying to teach us to be kind to each other and grateful to Him, go back and study it until you get it. It is a perfect document. The customary phrase is "Torah is truth."

If you cannot comprehend the Torah as the truth, I strongly suggest you study it until you comprehend every word as the truth. An immense number of very intelligent people have paved the way to understanding. I read many things as coming from an exasperated God.

The first of the five books of the Torah is Genesis, or Bereshis. This is the story from the garden of Eden through Abraham. It is the book that is imperative for all people. Genesis contains the first three covenants between God and humans on this planet to enable His plan for the garden of Eden.

Adam and Eve, as the first people in this civilization, chose the tree of knowledge. It applies to all individuals on this planet. It is not a religion. It is knowledge of good and bad and everything in between.

The Second Covenant, based on Noah, the Flood, and our common calendar, is also a universal paradigm. The calendar has a specific relationship to the sun and moon in seven-year periods.

The four other books apply to Jews as a nation specifically. They are all dated in the Age of Aries.

Their story is the tree of life. It was dormant in the garden of Eden until Jews accepted the Torah from God at Mount Sinai. This calendar is a nineteen-year cycle between the sun and moon.

Both trees are organizing systems incorporating time and human evaluative components. They are both based on human relationships and kindness. The tree of knowledge ascends *to* God with choices based on human interactions. The tree of life receives *from* God the rules for human interactions.

The primary distinction is that they create a permanent cycle, a double helix, that is intelligent and stable. They are not opposites but rather a pair creating a whole.

All people on this planet are connected to Genesis and specifically the first two covenants, which were made during the Age of Taurus.

All can study the other four books in the context of Genesis for their own guidance.

The remainder of the Tanach, which is largely similar to the Old Testament, is written by Jews in the context of the Torah as truth. Every thought refers back to the Torah for understanding and clarity. Some of the Tehillim, or Psalms, are written in the pattern of the Torah. These are by

Moses or King David to the best of my knowledge. They were following the pattern, but it is a matter of a few verses, not the entirety.

I totally believe Jesus taught the Way of Return. He was, in my understanding, the first person who taught the concept of the tree of knowledge as the path upward to God. Once I could get beyond the concepts of the Council of Nicea in the year 315 CE, I could recognize what Jesus taught. That is the subject of another book, *One Century, Twelve Jews*. Please understand I believe Jesus taught the Torah devotedly. He was dedicated to bringing Jews back to Judaism. He did not change Jewish beliefs whatsoever. It was only at the end of his mission that non-Jews joined. They were accepted as Jews. The disciples of Jesus were Jews. The apostles were not alive when Jesus taught. They came after the destruction of the second temple in the year AD 72. That is abundantly clear when anyone reads the books of the apostles: Matthew, Mark, Luke, and John. They discuss events and Judaism after the fall of the second temple and the resultant changes when followers of Peter and Paul discussed Seders in people's homes rather than in the temple. For their own preservation after the destruction of the temple, they began disassociation with the Jews.

Jesus was a gregarious, devout student at Beit Hillel, the School of Hillel, while Rabbi Hillel was still alive. He was not an Essene, which is often asserted. Essenes were a monastic, spiritual sect living in the desert. They were celibate and followed strict laws. He was not a member of the Saducees, the aristocrats. He certainly did not agree with those who sided with the Romans.

Many were connected to the Romans and have not carried forth into the Piscean Age. His twelve disciples were secularized Jews. He brought them back to observance.

He was, possibly, the first person to teach the tree of knowledge, and he taught action, not study. Jesus was an activist, not a scholar, and was dedicated to the common folks. When you consider Jesus and his teaching, you will see he was definitely concentrating on God as a verb.

In the sequel to this book, *The Way of Return on the Tree of Knowledge*, we illustrate his teachings with the Beatitudes. Once we get past the concepts taught by the Council of Nicea, Klal Israel, the Jews, and Jesus, a positive member of the Jewish community, we can look at both Jesus and Judaism as positive, constructive dynamics in our world. They become, in reality, a pair. The Jews have kept the tree of life, the laws of Moses, and Jesus, the Jew, has taught the Way of Return for all peoples on the tree of knowledge. The two streams are, in fact, a double helix, not opposites.

There is a good commentary in the Jewish Virtual Library about Jesus. When I began working with a Torah-based project, the biggest upset for me was the distortion of time and events in the New Testament. Read the book of James, the brother of Jesus. James is the only book by a practicing, observant (orthodox) Jew, who knew Jesus. The qualifying terms are most obviously added in the Council of Nicea. Peter, one of the disciples, returned to Judaism.

You can read through the lines that the brethren were secularized Jews. Understanding Jesus from the point of view that he taught the Way of Return led me to understand that all true prophets receive *from* God aligned on the tree of life. However, they teach the return. All teach the tree of knowledge in one way or another.

Consequently, this book is written for those who have strong opinions one way or another. It is a context to consider. It may well serve to spark a discussion among the Millennials, many of whom are atheists. My vantage point is to follow the patterns.

I look at this concept as a way of pairing the concepts of God, rather than those who think they have the only way. There is no single path back to God. We all have our own soul journey upward. We need all the knowledge and all the pairing possible.

This book is intended to provide clarity and understanding based on concepts in Genesis, particularly the garden of Eden. Once we have an intelligent basis for life on this planet with historical continuity, we can begin the process of alignment to the Age of Aquarius and thinking in terms of harmony and the brotherhood of all humankind.

Our lives are designed for our own personal return to God in harmony with others.

This book has as its primary context that a positive, purposeful God created the test of the garden of Eden so that humans would have made the choice to leave the heavenly realm provided for them in Eden. Thus, all people have the potential to return. They were not created with the obligation to return. That obligation would have negated the entire process for return.

Angels do God's bidding. They never have the opportunity for gratitude and response. God creates. God cannot respond to Himself. Others must do that.

God created us with the freewill choice and challenge to relate to each other with positive acts and loving-kindness.

This paradigm obliterates the concepts of the original sin and the Fall from grace. This planet is not based on punishment by God. The problem with texts written in the Piscean Age is they often separate and they delineate hierarchy. The challenge is to overcome the hierarchy.

Interestingly, working to reverse the "original sin" often results in acts of kindness and compassion. Pseudo-positive teachings regularly result in ego and acts of cruelty. The absolute absence of God is pure ego. God is a verb. God, therefore, does not have an ego. Our souls do not have an ego. Our ego is our free will, and the challenge is to keep our ego in harmony with our soul.

7

GOD'S AHA! — GOD CAN CREATE ANYTHING EXCEPT …

God can create anything and do anything except respond to Himself. He cannot demand gratitude or create a freewill choice to return. He cannot or chooses not to make humans be kind to each other. God cannot create a response, a reaction.

God has abundant imagination and wisdom and capability. His capacity to create is unlimited. He is creation. He can create anything—from the tiniest entities to the biggest and most complex. It all is orderly and intelligent.

Angels, archangels, and other heavenly beings can follow their instructions and purpose unconditionally. They do not have choice. In God's universe, the missing element, freewill choice, must come from others. That is the purpose of human beings on our planet Earth. We must choose to be kind and grateful to God and to our fellow human beings.

Angels are incredibly happy doing whatever God needs and wants. It is their purpose. From all we know, they always follow their purpose, be it a one-time event or a continuum for long periods.

When they succeed, both God and the angels are happy, but it was a mission, not a choice.

What God lacked was humans coming to Him out of free will in gratitude or in being kind to other human beings. It was flat. Somehow, sharing hard times is important, but if a necessity, it can be done alone. The difficult part is to be alone and have great good news or an event or circumstance without someone to share it with and respond to it. It is the commonality of joy that matters. God could not create a joyful reaction to Him.

He tried civilization after civilization on our planet in hopes they would be grateful. Civilization after civilization failed totally. There was no bond of joy, gratitude, and thanksgiving. It could be understood as a long-term chess game, where it was about wits, or a dollhouse, wherein God would move the dolls here and there.

Shared joy and appreciation were missing. God destroyed many civilizations trying to achieve a partnership of His creating with the people responding in awe and appreciation and with wonder and kindness to each other. He wanted humans to love each other as well and to be nice. He had so many failures, such as Lemuria and Atlantis. Currently, a dozen ruins from a dozen prehistoric destroyed civilizations have been identified. God kept starting over to no avail.

Then, God had a *huge aha*!

God kept creating humans on planet Earth with the hope they would be kind to others and be grateful. Civilization after civilization failed— totally. Then God had a big—*a super-big*—aha!

Humans needed a freewill choice to leave in order to have a freewill choice to return. They could not be expected to return if they had never made the choice to leave.

God then developed a plan for the garden of Eden, Adam and Eve. They would have perfect conditions. There was only one rule.

It was a very simple rule with no ambiguity: Do not eat from the tree of knowledge of good and bad. That meant knowledge of everything in between as well.

> And the Lord God commanded man, saying, "Of every tree of the garden you may freely eat. But of the Tree of Knowledge of good and evil you shall not eat of it, for on the day that you eat thereof, you shall surely die." (Genesis 2:16–17)

Humans had to make their own choice to leave in order to have their own freewill choice to return.

It is readily apparent that God would not have killed Adam and Eve. He was giving them a rule with consequences. Our positive God, the verb, would not have killed Adam and Eve for one transgression.

His larger plan was to get them to choose the tree of knowledge.

With them having made their own choice to leave, God could then proceed with His program for an eternal cycle of His acts of kindness, our gratitude, and, most important, our acts of kindness to each other. It is designed to be joyous.

He put it in action 5,778 years ago. It is a 6,000-year plan.

How are we doing?

God evidently wants to share joy with humans. It is a solitary thing to be doing good things for humans and not have a shared experience. He wants to share our joy, and He wants to share His joy!

I am giving my account of a seminal experience in my life. It has been valid for me ever since and has been the focal point of my decisions and actions. The event is not for anyone to judge. I accepted it and behave accordingly. I think if God wants to communicate, God uses the method most likely to succeed with each of us individually. Mine was 100 percent for me in retrospect. I have never heard of a similar situation, but it was for me and me alone.

In 1984, I had a profound mystical experience. There were witnesses. I was asked if I would release some of my free will in order to be useful to God doing that which He needed. I was taught the importance of making a vow with a ritual of my own choice. If I wanted to break my vow, I must make it clear with another ritual.

Breaking a vow responsibly is a rigorous mandate. Regardless of anything else in this, breaking a vow is one of the critical aspects for all of us. We are not locked into vows if we terminate them responsibly.

I was asked what I needed and wanted. I responded that everything had to be totally clear and right in front of me. I did not want to be concerned about what was needed. I also said I wanted to bring honor to my parents and facilitate their descendants.

God actually gave situations that were very clear and quite often in a set of three unrelated but aligned incidents within a short period of time. If I didn't pay attention to the signals, I got them in increasing intensity. The free will comes in everything that is outside my vow.

I was told I would not understand the purpose but with my attitude, God knew He could trust me.

Believe me; I had no idea why any of this was important. However, the part that was astounding, absolutely astounding, is that for the things I recognized at some point in the future, everything came together. Things that were totally obscure became clear. In most cases, these points of becoming obvious or finalized were hugely funny—funny beyond funny. It was never what I expected. I actually laughed with God! God made me laugh! I laughed at God's humor.

One very interesting aspect is that I cannot ever explain what was so uproariously funny. It is the result of complex experiences.

Furthermore, it vanishes as quickly as it comes. All I can say is that I have laughed with God. I have laughed so hard. I found God is very clever at assembling groups of actions. He finds or creates a common thread that mere mortals would never anticipate. All of a sudden, a group of events comes together when you least expect it. It is an outrageous surprise.

Is anyone laughing with God? Does anyone know or care that God is really very, very funny? It is certainly time to pay attention to God as humorous. It may be the very best thing.

God cannot laugh alone. Feedback is essential.

I think laughing with God is akin to seeing fire rainbows in the sky. They don't happen often, but it is an unforgettable experience.

My only advice comes from my experience. Do not ask for what you want. Ask, "Hey, God! What now?" Then listen.

These experiences have led me to have my own perspective on my relationship with God in accordance with God's purpose for humans on our planet.

God wants our partnership so that He can have the experience of relationship. God can most assuredly create anything. God needs us in order to have experience, any experience, of partnership and interaction. Our awe and gratitude are the beginning. Our treating others with kindness, compassion, justice, and awareness are the purposeful actions. To commune in good times as well as the sad is evidence of our humanness. Creative endeavors are most assuredly a delight to God. The aspects of a return to God are endless and all positive. God cannot create a freewill response, particularly in joy!

8

CHOOSING THE TREE
OF KNOWLEDGE

When putting Adam in the garden of Eden, God gave very clear instructions.

Bereshis (Genesis) 2:16–17 says, "And the Lord God commanded man, saying, 'Of every tree of the garden you may freely eat. But of the Tree of Knowledge of good and evil you shall not eat of it, for on the day that you eat thereof, you shall surely die.'"

Then Eve was created, and together, they chose to eat of the tree of knowledge. Knowledge implies understanding of good and bad as choices and the ability to discern the differences and similarities of the spectrum between them. There are no secrets.

The range is all-encompassing. Knowledge implies using our intelligence and factors available to us, such as experience, learning, and interacting with others during the process of life itself. The tree of knowledge is knowledge without limits, knowledge without bounds.

The significant aspect of the tree of knowledge is that it was the choice for a meaningful life based on possibilities. In the garden of Eden, all would be provided, and there were no obvious opportunities for personal growth. The tree of knowledge requires one's thoughts and active participation in one's own life.

The challenges of a life on the tree of knowledge with differentiations and distinctions, with possibilities, is far different from those of the angels, who do their missions happily and dutifully.

The angels do not have the joy of making decisions and improving matters for themselves and others. Do they have heartfelt gratitude to God for giving them a good task? Humans, since the garden of Eden, have the full range of opportunities to create a meaningful life with kindness and gratitude, compassion and joy.

We can live using the attributes God has and has made available for us. Within the garden of Eden, they might have had a perpetual childhood and innocence.

Was it really a bad choice to choose knowledge? Was it a bad choice to follow their curiosity? Was it a bad choice to make the huge decision together?

It is quite possible that if Adam and Eve had not chosen to eat the apple, their children most certainly would have. Their children would have been disobeying their parents as well as God.

That would have been dire for all times. God could have started over once again since his covenant with Noah had not happened.

Do understand the two covenants in Taurus do not create a religion. The purpose is relatedness to each other in kindness. Religions can use these just well as any philosophy or personal system. Religions are created by groups of humans and may apply these concepts knowingly or not.

9

TWO TREES IN GENESIS

The Tree of Life and
The Tree of Knowledge Showing the Way of Return

There were two trees in the garden of Eden: the tree of life and the tree of knowledge. However, in the book of Genesis, or Bereshis, the rule and the actions established the tree of knowledge and the Way of Return for all people. The tree of life was fallow until the Jews as a nation accepted the Ten Commandments and made the promise to teach them to their children in every generation.

> And HaShem said: "Shall I hide from Abraham that which I am doing; seeing that Abraham shall surely become a great and mighty nation, and all the nations of the earth shall be blessed in him?" (Genesis (Bereshis) 18:17–18)

Most religions have believed in *one supreme god*, whether stated directly or not. All teach some form of the golden rule to treat people with kindness and consideration at the core of their beliefs.

Three covenants in the book of Genesis (Bereshis) established the tree of knowledge and the Way of Return for all people on our planet.

Adam and Eve chose to leave the garden of Eden. It was their freewill choice, and they took with them the gift of the tree of knowledge, knowledge without limits, for every person on this planet, regardless of their recognition of the process of return.

The entire purpose of this six-thousand-year plan is to return to God with awe and appreciation of God and our fellow human beings. We do not proceed blindly since the first things Adam and Eve received were the gifts of sight and awareness. Compassion is key.

Genesis contains the stories to enable us to return to God with knowledge and applied values. The stories all can be read with positive, purposeful meaning.

Meanwhile, the tree of life is just lying dormant in the garden of Eden. Nothing happened with it during the entire book of Genesis.

Virtually every religion and teaching has the golden rule as a core component of its concepts. Jesus attended Brit Hillel, while Hillel was still alive. His primary teacher was one of the great holy rabbis. Hillel taught, "That which is distasteful to you, do not do to another." Jesus taught, "Do unto others as you would have them do unto you." Their versions are a perfect example of pairing.

Eastern religions have similar teachings with an implied return to God. The principles are consistent with the tree of knowledge. The stories of the garden of Eden and the deluge are found globally.

Consider that every human being has his or her own beam of light connected to God as the source. There is no right way to honor God and each other. It is everyone's freewill choice to find his or her own perfect path. The choices as to details are ours. God clearly has given options for an ethical choice for us all. There is no one religion or path that is better. Every single beam of light is a perfect manifestation of our connection to God. How we live is a direction of our own souls. It is always, always about pairing and harmony, leading to peace on our planet. We must follow our hearts and minds and most of all our souls, our innermost being, to treat God and others the very best we can.

Selah.

Muriel Rukeyser said, "The universe is composed of stories, not atoms."

10

THE FIRST COVENANT: ADAM AND EVE

God devised a plan for Adam and Eve to leave the garden of Eden by choice. He created a perfectly beautiful garden with everything they could need. He gave Adam one very simple rule: "Do not eat the apple from the tree of knowledge."

> And the Lord God commanded man, saying, "Of every tree of the garden you may freely eat. But of the Tree of Knowledge of good and evil you shall not eat of it, for on the day that you eat thereof, you shall surely die." (Genesis (Bereshis) 2:16–17)

Then God created Eve. They quickly justified eating the apple and did so.

Then the feminine voice of God, the Sheckinah, very softly spoke to them. Nonthreatening. Oops.

They could have approached God with some humility and asked for forgiveness. They could have asked for a second chance. They did not.

They didn't even try to save each other.
They broke the rule.
They had caused each other to do evil.
They blamed each other.
They lied.
They obviously did not respect God.

God banished them. This was His first judicial act. God was merciful. He did not kill them as they had been warned. He banished them.

This was, in fact, what He expected. It was what He wanted.

He had clear and certain conditions for a freewill choice to return to God in gratitude and acts of goodness. This was very straightforward.

What do we know about the tree of knowledge? First of all, Adam and Eve suddenly could think about what they saw. Instantly, they realized their bodies were different, and they clothed themselves. It was the first aspect of awareness. It was not about good or evil but rather a visual truth. Before they had knowledge, Adam and Eve obviously were stupid. They couldn't reason, and they saw nothing. They had no experience. It was no surprise to God that they ate an apple from the tree of knowledge. They literally knew nothing. They had not been tested, and they had not learned. The idea of having good advice or discussing it with God did not even register as a possibility.

When God gave knowledge, it was based on recognizing information. It was not a case of declaring opposites but rather realizing a pair, different-looking bodies. The tree of knowledge contains everything in between good and evil. It is knowledge without limits. It provides the conditions to create awareness and harmony, not opposite poles. Humans choose to make opposition and controversy rather than looking for peace.

Literally, our planet is not about separating everything according to the north and south poles but rather knowing everything in between with the purpose of informed choices.

When we raise our children, one of their first actions is to disobey just to prove themselves.

My granddaughter was not yet two years old, and she made her first stance for independence. She ran up the driveway away from me. I took a photograph since it was so purposeful. She got to the end of the driveway and stopped. She knew her own limits. She had more awareness than Adam and Eve. She had countless lessons and discoveries in her first years. She had knowledge and knew right from wrong immediately.

God giving Adam and Eve the admonition not to partake of the apple of knowledge was in the mind-set of a parent with small children. There is that stage when a toddler declares his or her independence of thought, word, and deed. Adam and Eve were at that stage since they were just formed, knew nothing, and had no experience. They could have been permanently in that state of being without knowledge and forethought. They chose to take a path that was based on making good choices. Their first choice was not good.

The first covenant with Adam and Eve ended with these words.

> And God said: "Behold, the man is become as one of us, to know good and evil; and now, lest he put forth his hand, and take also of the tree of life, and eat, and live for ever."

Therefore God sent him forth from the garden of Eden, to till the ground from whence he was taken.   So He drove out the man; and He placed at the east of the garden of Eden the cherubim, and the flaming sword which turned every way, to keep the way to the tree of life. (Genesis 2:22–24)

God clearly established that Adam and Eve had the tree of knowledge of good and evil permanently. Adam and Eve and all peoples on our planet have knowledge as part of our being.

There are no limits to our knowledge. This is indicated by including both good and evil and everything in between. As always, God creates in pairs with the potential for harmony. He does not say good or evil. He does not limit our knowledge.

We all learn to use our senses, our minds, and our experiences to live a meaningful life. We all have the potential to have knowledge as the basis for our entire life. We can learn from the past and the present and have an informed future. Access to knowledge and the ability to use it is our gift. How we use it is our decision.

Furthermore, He does not limit the access to the tree of life. It stood idle until the covenant with the Jews as a nation. It was always guarded for protection from damage, but it has been ours to use, as has the tree of knowledge. Jews have the obligation to adhere to the tree of life. All other individuals have access to the information in the tree of life as well as the tree of knowledge.

However, it is an entire system, whole and complete, which Jews live. Gentiles of all manner have the choice to return to God and have the option to use the tree of knowledge in a positive, constructive life path. It is a freewill choice without a directive. In our sequel, we will teach the tree of knowledge as an adaptation of the tree of life used to return to God.

Adam and Eve and all their descendants have been given every aspect possible to help us on our Way of Return. There are no restrictions on that which we receive and use. There are no limitations on our minds and experiences. We all have the potential for a freewill choice to return to God with gratitude and acts of kindness.

Adam and Eve chose to leave the garden of their own volition. They did not even consider the potential for wisdom implied by the tree of life. The freewill choice to leave enabled a freewill choice to return.

Together, they chose to eat of the tree of knowledge. Knowledge implies understanding of good and bad as choices and the ability to discern the differences and similarities of the spectrum between them. There are no secrets. The range is all-encompassing. Knowledge implies using our intelligence and factors available to us, such as experience, learning, and interacting with others during the process of life itself.

The significant aspect of the tree of knowledge is that it was the choice for a meaningful life based on possibilities. In the garden of Eden, all would be provided, and there were no obvious opportunities for personal growth. The tree of knowledge requires one's thoughts and active participation in one's own life.

The challenges of a life on the tree of knowledge with differentiations and distinctions, with possibilities, are far different from those of angels, who do their missions happily and dutifully.

The angels do not have the joy of making decisions and improving matters for themselves and others. Do they have heartfelt gratitude to God for giving them a good task? Humans, since the garden of Eden, have the full range of opportunities to create a meaningful life with kindness and gratitude.

The most obvious aspect of the trees is that taking any component out of the context of the tree of life puts it in a different paradigm. Therefore, the validity is subject to scrutiny. We can live using the attributes God has and has made available for us. Within the garden of Eden, they might have had a perpetual childhood and innocence.

Was it really a bad choice to choose knowledge? Was it a bad choice to follow their curiosity? Was it a bad choice to make the huge decision together?

Lynn Keller

It is quite possible that if Adam and Eve had not chosen to eat the apple, their children most certainly would have. Their children would have been disobeying their parents as well as God.

God could have started over once again since His covenant with Noah had not happened.

11

THE SECOND COVENANT: NOAH

God wanted humans to have a level playing field for the return. He wanted to eliminate problems of genetics, stories, and enemies stemming from peoples from prior civilizations. In addition, there had been virtually no progress from descendants of Adam and Eve.

As time went by, there was no progress toward a return to God based on kindness and gratitude. There just was little intention to be nice to others. Noah, however, was doing well with his family. God assigned Noah the task of building a huge boat on the top of a mountain. The purpose was to save Noah and his family and sets of animals.

Noah even had to lug trees since the mountain was so high. It took 120 years. The whole time, Noah's neighbors jeered at him.

Noah just trusted God since it didn't make sense. It was a tough job, and the neighbors made it worse.

Finally, Noah gathered his family and all the animals, and the deluge came. As we know, it rained hard for forty days. It covered the mountain.

The surprising thing to Noah was that he missed all the folks who had been taunting him. He did not like the void in companionship. He asked God never to destroy people again. "Please don't give up on people." God agreed.

God sent the sign of a dove. He has kept His word. It must have been very tempting at times to just get rid of everybody and start again. We can all note times when God could have decided to just scrub this experiment. He had numerous times before the covenant with Adam and Eve, when He destroyed civilizations. God also sent Noah the Jubilee calendar to track the seven-day cycles with the seventh day each week spent in joy and relationship with each other. Clearly, relatedness was the key component in the purpose of human beings on this planet.

While Noah offered this covenant to God, there is every reason to think that God knew from previous civilizations that there would be reasons to get rid of the entire civilization.

At this point, we need help to save our planet as well as our civilization.

God accepted; He has kept His word.
God has never wavered as we know.

12

THE WAY OF RETURN: PATTERNS AND PURPOSE GIVEN IN THE AGE OF TAURUS

In the Age of Taurus, we were given a clear purpose and the tools we need to be in alignment with each other and God.

Adam and Eve made a choice to follow their will and begin relatedness. They had the tree of knowledge, which is an organized system of integrated thinking, being, and actions for ourselves and others. It begins with self-awareness and continues through learned traits and connectivity based on how we treat each other. In so doing, we show the awe and appreciation of God, knowingly or not.

With Noah came our standard calendar to enable inclusion of time in a very extended period. It may well be that groups such as Native Americans had flourishing communities and belief systems, but they lacked long-term markers.

Noah's Jubilee calendar set a yearly cycle of seven-day periods with a celebration with others as the final day. The final day, the Double Jubilee day, was a separate method of counting the patterns.

The tree of knowledge and Noah's Jubilee calendar are integrated to facilitate our relatedness with each other as a primary goal.

These two covenants establish basic principles and standards of behavior toward each other.

Taurus is considered bucolic. The focus was on living in and as a community. Our six-thousand-year period, based on relatedness, began then.

Never forget that Noah asked God never to destroy people again. He missed his friends, regardless of their jeering. The calendar with each seventh day being one of jubilee and celebration with each other was an aspect of relatedness for the people.

13

THE THIRD COVENANT: ABRAHAM

In order to establish the return to God, it was mandatory to establish there was *one God*, holy, supreme, and eternal.

Over the centuries, the population spread, but there was considerable paganism, worshiping many gods, animals, and things. The whole purpose for humans on planet Earth was to have a thriving return to God demonstrated though acts of kindness.

There was idolatry everywhere, but no one was showing gratitude to God. It was time for a demonstration of respect, appreciation, and trust in God, the one, true, positive, compassionate god.

The man who was at the highest level was Abraham. God chose Abraham to show his loyalty and trust of God. It seems there were sacrifices of all manner at that point. They were made to all manner of animals, gods, and objects—a very large number of things. *Nouns.*

It was time for drastic proof that God was the one true absolute God. Whoa!

Abraham was asked to sacrifice his beloved son, Isaac. Isaac agreed.

There are endless interpretations regarding this covenant. Consider this story with respect to God is a verb and that God always creates in pairs, not opposites. First of all, they both knew. The story of the great heroism to follow God unquestioningly was agreed upon and carried out by both father and son. Second, it tested them at the core of their being. They were tested at their essential natures.

Abraham was tested in his compassion and Isaac in his integrity. They were tested as a pair, and they succeeded together.

Lynn Keller

While there is no way to really understand the reason this was proof to God of their undeviating gratitude and respect for God, we do understand God's response, unwavering loyalty to Abraham and Isaac, which continues.

In a world filled with pagans, Abraham trusted God unconditionally and agreed to sacrifice his beloved son, Isaac. Fortunately, God just wanted a wholehearted agreement and sent a scapegoat for the sacrifice.

So there was another trip up a mountain to connect with God. Isaac was bound and about to be killed. All of a sudden, a small goat appeared. In the nick of time, it became the "scapegoat" as a substitute for Isaac.

Being willing to make this sacrifice was proof enough for God that there could be monotheism on this planet. Abraham was promised as many descendants as there were stars in the sky.

14

CHOOSING THE TREE
OF KNOWLEDGE

The choice to leave the garden of Eden, the agreement with God never to destroy people again, and the demonstration of faith in the One and Only God, who is a verb, established the context for human beings on our planet. There are no stories known to have preceded these covenants. Should any be found to have existed, they did not serve as the instructions for human beings throughout all these generations. For almost six thousand years, these teachings have been followed consecutively.

As far as I am aware, all Native American and Eastern religions and teachings fit this context. There are no separate or distinct gods that create a new paradigm. Instead, the basic concepts fit a supreme being without identifying the attributes or qualities.

The three covenants are all aligned to the tree of knowledge of all things and correspond to an orderly, purposeful return to God.

The format of the tree of knowledge with the return to God in gratitude and compassion can be used to organize, comprehend, and compare ethical systems. This is most obvious with the Abrahamic religions, such as Islam and Christianity, and the Greek teachings.

Since the tree of knowledge is an open, stable, multidimensional format, it is basic to countless sets of data and ideas. The distinction between the two trees is the direction to or from God.

Adam and Eve, progenitors for our planet for the last 5,700 years, established the choice to return to God. Jews accepted the covenant of Torah, the first five books of the Bible, pledging their descendants through every generation to adhere to the teachings as instructed by God. This is the tree of life, and it is a mandatory component of the double helix composed of the two trees. Jews have a choice within the covenant, but their mandate is clear and certain. They must accept the rules of the tree of life and teach it to their children. By living according to the lightning flash from the feminine aspect of God, they enable the double helix to be upheld on our planet.

Both trees must be in effect to enable a continuous, stable, and organized flow of relationship with God and all people on our planet.

The third covenant with Abraham established that there is one god. The concept of a sole deity was introduced in the Age of Aries. God, a single creative force, creates in pairs, not opposites, and has no differentiation or separation within Himself. God, our creator, is a total oneness, a verb. In the Age of Taurus, humans were created to be connected to one another in acts and thoughts of kindness. These acts reflect our freewill choice, and, thus, we respond and reflect back to our One True God with awe and appreciation.

There are not multiple gods. God is unity itself. God is a verb in thought, creation, and action.

15

THE FOURTH COVENANT: THE TEN COMMANDMENTS

Jacob's dream of the angels going up and down the ladder indicated the double helix.

God, in His determination to have the garden of Eden trial succeed on planet Earth, had one further critical element to put in place. In the garden of Eden, Adam and Eve had eaten an apple from the tree of knowledge of good and evil. Thus, the Way of Return for everyone on the planet has been aligned to that tree. Each person on this planet was required to make his or her own positive choices in the return to God in awe and appreciation, in doing acts of kindness and in showing respect for God.

One might imagine God as a source of light and love, emitting a beam of light to each of us, a ray of sunshine to all people, so they have their own direct connection to God. We all have the potential to freely choose our path and keep our own light shining.

God decided that He must have a stream separately coming down through a group of people who would have pledged their children throughout eternity to live according to God's rules. Descendants of Isaac were chosen most likely because of his willingness to be sacrificed to the *one true God*.

This pattern of two trees is the fundamental aspect of God's plan to have humans return in a freewill choice. The significant aspect that is overlooked is that the two trees actually comprise a double helix of a pair of trees. The trees contain similar but not exact formations and have different streams or sources of data and stories.

Jacob, in his dream, actually envisioned the angels ascending and descending on the ladder while he wrestled with the negative force.

His dream depicted the double helix of the two trees. There were two streams, two directions connected to God. Thus, the two trees in the garden of Eden are established as a system on our planet Earth.

Many centuries later, after enslavement in Egypt and time in the desert, Jews were led to Mount Sinai to hear God. "Led" is a gentle word. Actually God held a mountain over their heads. The Jews had to promise to give their children to God in order to receive His Word.

There had to be a permanent, stable group or nation to receive God's word unconditionally. Within the covenant, they had free will, but it required absolute allegiance to the Torah, the five books, and to doing acts of kindness as directed by God. Thus, they live the tree of life. As a nation, they are bound to receive from God His instructions and mandates.

What happens to those Jews who leave the covenant? They leave by their own choice. Logically, they become aligned to all others on the tree of knowledge of good and evil.

The fourth covenant establishes the plan created in the garden of Eden as the operating system for people on our planet. Jews, as a nation, accepted the Ten Commandments. These are the rules as given by God to create a living model through every generation. By adhering to God's guidebook, Jews connect the tree of life to planet Earth.

There is no indication that any attempt before the garden of Eden established a cogent ethical system on our planet. The four covenants established the organizing system for all the peoples on this planet.

And God said: "Behold, the man is become as one of us, to know good and evil; and now, lest he put forth his hand, and take also of the tree of life, and eat, and live for ever."

Therefore God sent him forth from the garden of Eden, to till the ground from whence he was taken.

So He drove out the man; and He placed at the east of the garden of Eden the cherubim, and the flaming sword which turned every way, to keep the way to the tree of life. (Genesis 3:22–24)

The two trees establish a pair, designed to enable an ethical system on this planet. Both are positive, and both are necessary. This pair is totally consistent with the ways God has established a free return to God in acts of kindness and gratitude to all.

16

THE TWO TREES IN GENESIS: A DOUBLE HELIX

Selah.
Consider two trees as two spirals
Complementary and parallel
Going in opposite directions
Jews as a nation receive
From God according to the
Downward path on the tree of life.
Since the garden, all individuals have the choice to
return to God in an upward spiral on the tree of
knowledge, containing knowledge without limits.

God created two trees in the garden of Eden, and they have become the metaphor, the analogy for the operating system of our planet. It is a double helix, an organized, open, stable system, for all the peoples on our planet. The purpose is to live freely and kindly with each other and be in gratitude to God.

There are many Ways of Return. There have been many prophets. Arguably, every prophet who is aligned to the Way of Return has received instructions and information through the tree of life. Prophets receive *from* God and teach the Way of Return in awe and gratitude. All teach some form of the golden rule. Thinking that one is better than another is just a miscalculation and a separation from the double helix and, most of all, from God and our purpose for being.

The concept of knowledge of good and bad actually means knowledge without limits. It includes everything between good and bad. God does not create opposites. This is a pair that is inclusive.

It is up to all people individually to make the choice for themselves on values and information.

It is important to understand that Jesus, a religious, observant, passionately gregarious Jew, taught the Way of Return to secularized Jews. The primary teachings we have from him directly are the Beatitudes. He taught the Torah with simplicity and accuracy and studied at Beit Hillel. He did not add to or change the Torah. He was an activist, not a scholar. He may well have been the first person who taught the Way of Return on the tree of knowledge.

There are now many ways of return that are established or personal. They have in common the golden rule in one form or another. Most have a concept of the Supreme Intelligence Creator. It is the alignment to the tree of knowledge of good and evil that Adam and Eve chose—freely chose.

Are there communities that preexisted the garden of Eden? If any remain, they have been peacemakers and have not spread their teachings beyond their communities. They have always lived on the Way of Return.

The critical verse is Genesis 18:18: "All the nations of the world shall be blessed in him."

This clearly establishes a Way of Return for all people. Most religions have had a prophet who believed in One Supreme God and taught some form of the golden rule and gratitude. Consider that every human has his or her own beam of light connected to God. There is no "right" way to honor God and each other. It is everyone's choice to find his or her own perfect path. The choices as to details are ours. God clearly has given choices for an ethical life for all.

However, the tree of life was not put actively in place until Mount Sinai when the Jews as a nation agreed to abide directly by the Word of God.

In the book of Genesis 2:9, we read, "And out of the ground made the Lord God to grow every tree that is pleasant to the sight, and good for food; the tree of life also in the midst of the garden, and the tree of the knowledge of good and evil."

To make this clear, the tree of knowledge was identified specifically for Adam, Eve, and all people to adhere to thereafter. It is knowledge without limits. The tree of life was activated by the Jews as a nation. It was Jews as a group.

The double helix of the two trees was started with one helix when Adam and Eve were banished. The tree of life was instigated as a result of the covenant at Mount Sinai.

Abraham established one God for all his generations. Muslims are conscious about the tree of knowledge. His descendants, through Hagar and Ketura, as well as Esau and other children, are all gentiles and follow the tree of knowledge, the Way of Return.

Because of their vow, descendants of Jacob established the tree of life. It came into action long after the tree of knowledge of good and evil. It was lying fallow until the nation of Israel was formed by acceptance of the Ten Commandments and pledging their children throughout every generation.

It is a matter of pairs, not a hierarchy, on our planet. God is supreme, and He works with pairs in creation. The nation of Israel is not better or worse than those of gentiles. It is a mandatory component of the return to God on our planet and for all people. Both trees are necessary. God has created an open, stable design for the human beings on our planet. There are two trees, and they operate as a double helix, compatible but going in opposite directions. Once again, the two trees were designed as a pair. It means knowledge without limits on the tree of knowledge and knowledge as a standard on the tree of life according to the fourth covenant. They are a pair to establish peace on our planet.

The binding of Isaac in the book of Genesis solidly placed the tree of knowledge of good and bad on our planet. It is an organizing system for the freewill choice to return to God. No other teachings exist that predate this process. If a fragment of teachings was ever found, it was useful for study, but it made no impact on the last 5,778 years.

During the entire period of Genesis, the tree of life lay dormant. The gates protected the garden, and it was open to all. However, no one came. God, as is consistent with all God does, had a plan.

It was, of course, two trees. The plan was to have the tree of knowledge be the basis for the return to God with a freewill choice for kindness and gratitude. The tree of life was coming from God as an eternal source of kindness and order.

The model is the double helix of DNA. It is composed of two counterparallel spirals going in opposite directions.

In effect, the tree of life comes *down* from God directly, and the tree of knowledge is the return *to* God.

The next four books of the Torah are the story of putting the tree of life in action through the nation of Jews. The story from Isaac to the giving of the Ten Commandments and the last day of Moses's life is decisively about Jews as a nation accepting this system. They pledged their descendants through eternity. The rules are specifically to live according to the tree of life. All the teachings are available to everyone. Jews, however, live it as a system with dedication. They receive from God the instructions. There is no debate.

Jews receive.
Gentiles return.

The tree of life comes down.
The tree of knowledge goes up.

This can be understood as God designing and creating in complementary pairs. They are designed to be in equilibrium.

17

THE FIRST TWO COMMANDMENTS

As lists go, the Ten Commandments are essentially universal. Yet from the written word of the Bible, how many of us even know there is no agreement as to what they are? Jews, Catholics, and Protestants are totally committed to their own versions.

The significant differences are in the first two commandments. Given that God gives us information in patterns and with repetition, these two commandments show the clear and certain differences in the tree of life and the Way of Return.

The first two commandments were given directly by God to the Jews in the process of their becoming a nation. God delivered these two commandments in a thundering voice that frightened the Jews to the core of their being. There were two million Jews there, and God's message and purpose were quite clear. God communicated verbally and directly. Arguably, nothing else has mattered more to that extent.

They had centuries of hard slavery, the plagues, and wandering through the desert, and they pledged their children for eternity to hear this. It was unbearably loud—thundering beyond anything we can imagine. The remaining commandments were communicated by Moses. There is no doubt as to God's intention to make certain these two commandments are a unit, separate and distinct.

The differences between the Jews and the Christians is not the words, but how they are communicated and placed in the set of ten.

One of God's primary patterns is to divide one into a pair of two. The two are always separate but equal. They are created to be a set for unity and equilibrium.

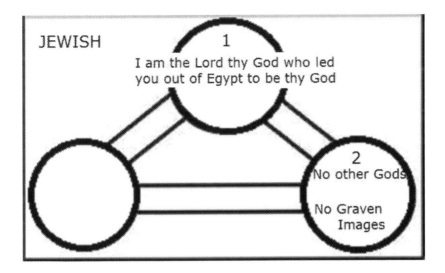

There is no doubt these two commandments were delivered in exactly this manner with this intent. This is the pattern for the tree of life. Arguably, the tree of life, which had been resting in the garden of Eden was activated by God's delivering these two commandments.

Throughout Torah, every verse is in this pattern of one explained by the next two. It is a document of total order and accord.

Following are the Jewish, Catholic, and Protestant versions of these two commandments. The order makes no sense unless you are on the tree of knowledge returning to God. Then both versions are valid.

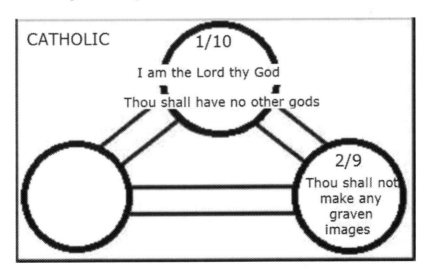

In the Catholic version, the first commandment includes the first part of the pair. God does not work in that manner. He starts with one and divides into two, a pair. It is different, and it makes sense as the Way of Return. It is not a system. It is a human choice.

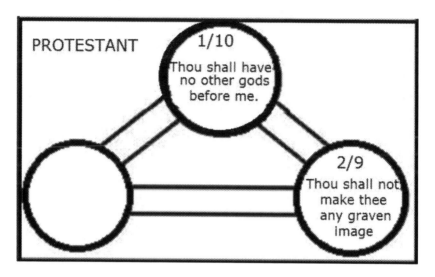

In the Protestant version, the first commandment is eliminated, and the second becomes two separate commandments. Apparently, God is above.

The Jews were there and probably overwhelmed by the intensity and volume of God's voice. God adamantly presented Himself so there would never be a question about His authenticity. Know who I Am! It is a complete thought and provides the context for all that follows.

The second commandment has two parts in alignment with the verses regarding the two trees in the garden of Eden. The other pattern, as noted, is the entire format of the Torah as one verse followed by two as indicators. It is the basic pattern of creation.

Both the Catholic and Protestant versions are perfectly aligned with the tree of knowledge for the Way of Return. There is an organized format designed as a counterparallel system to the tree of life. Every person must create his or her own way of return. It is an individual, freewill, voluntary process. The tree of knowledge of good and bad can be used at will. It is, of course, knowledge of all manners.

The return does not have the aspect of creation and division into pairs. It is an ascent, one step at a time.

18

REPETITION AND PATTERNS

God teaches us through patterns and through repetition. There is every indication that if we do not get our priorities and our lessons properly, we shall repeat them—quite possibly for many lifetimes.

Probably, it is even with the same soul groups or families—same lesson, over and over. As a family historian, I have been able to see patterns of my family in this lifetime paralleling those in generations before.

The pattern of the two verses regarding the two trees in Genesis is very clear. There is one verse that is a whole followed by a verse of concept that is dual. The same pattern is in the first two commandments. The whole of the Torah, the five books, is written entirely with the same pattern. Each verse is followed by the next two verses as an explanation or consideration. The pattern is analogous.

The verses in Genesis 2:16–17 are a set. The first verse states the garden as whole. The second is specific, regarding the tree of knowledge of good and evil. The second verse has two connected concepts: good and evil. The pattern of the two trees and the symbol of the two trees correspond directly.

These two verses are critical to understanding the Torah, which was written in a perfect mathematical sequence. Each verse is explained by the following two verses. Anyone can check as to the meaning by just following the pattern, each and every time. It is beyond the capability of human minds to conceive of such geometric patterns, much less achieve them. It is a sign of God's connection to us though His Holy Word.

God's giving of the first two commandments audibly is a congruent pattern. The first commandment is followed by one that has two parts.

First Commandment
"I am the Lord, your God, Who took you out of the land of Egypt, out of the house of bondage."

Second Commandment
"You shall not have the gods of others in My presence. You shall not make for yourself a graven image or any likeness which is in the heavens above, which is on the earth below, or which is in the water beneath the earth."

The process parallels cell division. One separates into two. They are pairs, designed to work in harmony, not opposition.

We learn from this pattern of the two trees and the second commandment that creation was division into pairs, not opposites. Opposites are an extreme differentiation of pairs. Opposites are not the general rule and are difficult to achieve. Polarization requires intention and dedication to achieve. Denial of the opposite requires rigid determination. Distinctions, similarities, and commonalities are the function of the two trees.

"Good" and "evil" can be either polar opposites or a pair that includes knowledge of everything in between.

Twos Show Differentiation

Pairs cooperate, unify, collaborate, look for commonality, partnerships, and togetherness. We and our opposites separate, divide, are hierarchical, and maintain our individuality and distinctions—adamantly!
They are *apart*ners. You and I are clear.

The relationship of two joining or dividing determines all other connections.

The most basic aspect is *ego*. Does your ego dominate and differentiate in your decisions and actions.

Polarization largely is the result of ego.

Apartner Words Polarize

Positive—Negative
Good—Bad
Right—Wrong
Mine—Yours
Best—Worst

Is the comparison from ego and judgment, or is it from balance and harmony?

Together is a wonderful distinction.

"Positive thinking" cults are particularly focused on apartner concepts. They limit knowledge and understanding in their passion to always state an "affirmation." They specifically do not allow high-quality data or information or experience. "You are telling me a story," said a minister. "Stop it! I will pray for you, but you must never call me again." I wanted resolution that was critical. Instead, I received an "affirmation" by rote. They are, in reality, mental manipulations. They are pronouncements, not affirmations in any way.

Selah—any computation based on insufficient data is always faulty.

In their cases, "There are two sides to everything" means they are totally polarized and never make a responsible decision. They are regularly very hurtful indeed. They are never appropriate. Realistically, anyone can see they are eliminating contacts and communication outside of their own control group. They deny intelligence in their interactions.

We learn from scientists that any computation based on insufficient data is *always* faulty. People who do not allow sufficient high-quality life have no way to make any decision or statement that is not egocentric. The unbelievable concept that "There are two sides to everything" is passionately against God, who is truth. If you do not know and do not care about determining truth, you will always have an extreme void in data, experience, and, most of all, truth.

These pseudo-positivity people are controlling and dictatorial and create extreme negativity by never allowing our hearts, minds, and instincts to deal with circumstances and information that is paramount to being appropriate. They are hugely separated from the Way of Return.

Actually, they can never be useful *to* God because they only tell God what they want. They do not listen to God or to others. Their "affirmations" are the best example of being *off the way of return*. In my experience, I think of my interactions with these folks and realize they have the ultimate self-vested interest priorities.

They have no humility. They never, ever consider, "Is this nice?" Pseudo-positivity people are the penultimate *apart*ners. They are the icon of separation.

The actuality is that anyone who thinks there is but one way to God is an apartner. Anyone demanding his or her own religion for others is the most clearly separated from God. Fortunately, our founding fathers recognized the danger of religious mandates and created our constitution with a dedication against the mixing of church and state. They were quite adamant not to include the practices from Europe.

Resolution and rectification of all kinds are the essence of *"pair"* thinking rather than opposites. These acts of kindness are critical in the Way of Return.

We all have a litany of phrases that have caused instant separation. They certainly do not need to be elucidated.

Healing words lead to pairs and pairing, not apartners and opposites. Some examples include the following:

- I'm sorry; I didn't think.
- I never thought.
- I didn't know.
- It never occurred to me.
- Tell me what happened.
- Tell me what you think.
- What can I do to help?
- What do your children need?
- What do you need?

The list of soft words with kind thoughts is endless. Every word matters.

The intention matters. There is a wonderful Japanese teaching: "Seicho No Ie." One of their teachings is to always repeat "Thank you."

"Arigato. Arigato gozaimas." (Thank you. Thank you very much.)

People get the second statement to a magnified degree. They pay attention.

The same policy works for an apology: "I'm sorry. I'm really very sorry." Children learn this well.

We are taught that all things are possible in the realm of God, except the awe and appreciation of God. God grants us the capacity for a freewill choice to return to God through awe, appreciation, and gratitude. However, the major criteria are how we treat others. Positive, purposeful relationships with others are, arguably, the purpose for human life on our planet.

From the reaction received from Japanese people upon hearing "Arigato gozaimas," I would venture that learning to say, "Thank you," in other languages is a wonderful way to be on the Way of Return *easily*! Repeating it is an immediate positive connection.

"Aloha" in the Hawaiian language means affection, peace, compassion, and mercy. Nowadays, it is also used for "hello" and "good-bye." It is, perhaps, the best word for the Way of Return. Say it often.

19

PATTERNS

As Bob Dorough wrote in *Schoolhouse Rock*, "Three is a magic number."

> It takes three legs to make a tripod
> Or to make a table stand.
> Every triangle has three corners,
> Every triangle has three sides,
> No more, no less.
> You don't have to guess.
> When it's three, you can see
> It's a magic number.

Until there are three, there is no form, no pattern.
Once is happenstance. Twice is a coincidence. Three is a pattern.
Once is a dot. Twice is a line. Three times
make a shape, a pattern, a form.

God, a verb, with infinite oneness with no boundaries and no parts,
has no patterns.
God creates patterns.
God creates an infinite number of patterns.
The patterns begin with three aspects.

In a lecture, Buckminster Fuller showed how stable a triangle is. His triangle could not be adjusted. It was a fixed form. He had a four-sided model with movable corners. Indeed, they could be shifted all sorts of ways. He was quite disparaging and dramatically threw it across the floor. Triangles are a major aspect of his work, including the geodesic dome.

Patterns beyond those having three aspects go on with more numbers, but three is the very basic form and set, a design. Three dots can make a pattern but not one. Two go every which way but cannot create a stable pattern or form. Two dots connected make one line.

It is extremely elementary but essential in recognizing God in action.

Obviously, the three sides can vary in length, and the three angles always add to 180, half the degrees in a circle. We all learn that early in grade school. Are we taught the significance in all groups of three?

We go one with four to make a shape with dimensions and then on to time. The important aspect of time is that it is not at all linear. It is in cycles and circles.

The two trees are integrated, orderly, intelligent systems. They are multifaceted and multidimensional. They coordinate sets of data into a comprehensible relationship model. They can be spheres and helixes, as well as a two-dimensional drawings. The second book in this set explains the tree of knowledge as the pattern for the Way of Return.

Buckminster Fuller taught that triangles are the building blocks of the universe. Certainly, his work shows that concept repeatedly.

Are triangles, with their rigid structure, the reason our universe does not collapse?

If you can clearly connect back to a point of time, the beginning, the origin, of any person, concept, or activity, you create a pattern. You create a dynamic that includes past, present, and future. It is a pattern of three. If you can connect back, you can establish the basis for a much stronger process. It is the set of three aspects that can propel a running leap into the future.

The trick is that you must have all issues resolved to get back to the beginning. Otherwise, you are founding your process on an incomplete situation. It is the resolution that enables a healthy vault forward. Otherwise, you are stuck in the muck and mire or proceed from a standstill.

Vaulting
When we connect back clearly and cleanly to the roots, to
the source of any idea or project, we get a profound impetus
forward into completion and into the future.

Any person who curtails resolution for another person has created an enormous block. It may be one of our greatest failures personally. Often, people are taught to just go forth and eliminate the past. That very well may be a huge block for the others involved. One must go back to the onset of any disagreement or great disharmony and attempt completion. It very well may be that we are judged in the truth process at the end of our lives by how well we have completed events for ourselves and others.

At the very least, all the incompletions block vaulting into the future. We can only go back to a clear and certain past to get a leap forward. Remember, patterns do not have to be physical. Patterns are evident in all our thoughts, words, deeds, and personal attributes.

Patterns are a priority. Look for similarities in things that seem different and differences in things that seem similar. Making the distinctions in patterns makes a tremendous impact on all your choices.

Everyone else, including Jews who separated from the clan, must return on the tree of knowledge, whether they recognize it or not.

Stop! Look! Listen!

20

TIME

Time is composed of an incredible variety of cycles and patterns. Time is not linear and goes in numerous directions.

A Day (capitalized) may be as long as an eon.

No cycle is a straight line. Reverse arrows of time are a significant aspect of life on our planet. There are many ways to measure time, but other than a calendar, time is nonlinear. It is always in cycles and goes forward and connects to the past.

The first aspect of time is found in Genesis and the days it took God to create components of our universe and our planet specifically. One day of twenty-four hours makes no sense cosmologically. It is a matter of understanding distinctions. A Day, capitalized, is eons long. A day, lowercased, is twenty-four hours. Both apply to periods of time without clarification.

The Torah itself is written without linear order. It will not make sense until you recognize you are connecting situations and circumstances.

There is an endless number of cycles in God's universe. There are a few that are of interest in this book.

The Mayan calendar is valid, yet the civilization is long gone and along with it, all continuity for that civilization going forward into our time. It speaks to the concept that God gave up on people until this two-thousand-year experiment wherein the people chose to leave. Therefore, a valid return is enabled.

Jupiter has a twelve-year cycle around the sun, whereas the cycle of Venus is shorter than that of the Earth. We see in astronomical data that they are at the same point about once a year. The significant qualification is that they are at the same point of longitude and latitude once in about two thousand years. When they are exactly aligned, the illumination is extraordinary. It is often explained by showing one candle exactly behind another. The light is magnified to a massive extreme. It happened about 6 BCE. I believe that was the Star of Bethlehem. The three wise men were astrologers from the Far East.

The very next occurrence was in August 2005. It was the time of Hurricane Katrina, followed by another. Both made a right-angle turn—one to New Orleans and one to East Texas. Arguably, that was the onset of the Age of Aquarius. There are many theories. This is the one I accept at this point.

Selah. Are we in the Age of Aquarius? In the year 6 BCE, there was a conjunction of Jupiter and Venus, which created an incredibly bright light. Quite possibly, it was the Star of Bethlehem. The very next conjunction of this pair was August 29, 2005, when we had Hurricane Katrina.

There are differences between the ages. The Piscean Age is depicted as two fish swimming in opposite directions. That is a remarkable icon since concepts in the Piscean Age are always opposites and differences rather than pairs and similarities to create harmony. Reflect on this possibility. *Selah.*

The six-thousand-year cycle beginning with Adam and Eve started in Taurus. What better story could represent the Age of Taurus than that of the garden of Eden! Taurus is the time frame for Genesis.

The other four books of the Torah, which are dedicated to Jews accepting the covenant from God directly, occur in the Age of Aries.

There is a full range of stories that befit this time. The enslavement of the Jews and the plagues are perfect Age of Aries happenings. The receiving of the Torah shows the promise that comes from Aries as the completion of a rotation of ages.

Ages happen in a clockwise order. Smaller cycles within the ages, such as years of our earth around our sun, rotate counterclockwise. That is an astronomical determination. It fits the order God has established to have cycles in two directions. The Piscean Age started not only the Age of Pisces but a new period of twelve ages.

Perhaps time in the universe is a double helix, as are the patterns on our planet. I do not know of any straight line in nature.

Our current counting of years began at approximately the onset of the Piscean Age. Most certainly, the problems began with the Romans asserting their dominance. The extreme violence of the first century of the Piscean Age was horrific. From my vantage point, we are in another exacerbated time now as the ages are shifting. Our very planet needs full cooperation and understanding in order for us to survive. It is no longer about obtaining a position of superiority but rather finding common accord.

As information to consider, the transfer into Pisces has proven to be focused on opposites, whether they be personal or biblical. It is always about the opposition, hierarchy, rankings, and polarizing. It is about separation and distinctions. The context that one religion is the only religion leads always into factions and fractures. The glyph shows the arcs facing in opposite directions. That has been the context for two millennia.

The glyph for Aquarius shows balance and harmony. There are corresponding parallel waves. The natural accord is self-evident.

Consider the depictions of fish. In Pisces, there are two fish going in opposite directions. In Aquarius, a school of fish swim in harmony and order. There is a common accord. One can observe, amid all the conflict and the fierce fighting, it is about rights rather than dominance and superiority.

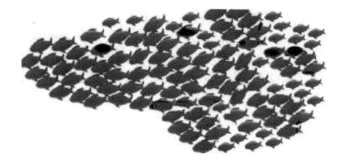

The lyrics from the musical *Hair* for the Age of Aquarius still reverberate.

> Harmony and understanding
> Sympathy and trust abounding
> No more falsehoods or derisions
> Golden living dreams of visions

We are entering the new paradigm.

In both the tree of life and the tree of knowledge without limits, the format is an open, stable system based on attributes of God that are achievable by humans. God has only positive characteristics and actions. There is no ego in God whatsoever. Therefore, our focus in the Age of Aquarius is to be in harmony with others in kindness and gratitude and to be in an eternal positive cycle and interactive relationship with God.

All of us observe cycles of the sun in a year, a week, or a month. We observe cycles of the moon as well. There are innumerable cycles. All have meaning.

A simple cycle is found in the relationship between the sun and moon. It takes nineteen years for the sun and moon to be in the exact same relationship. Thus for each of us, a new cycle begins every nineteen years. It is easy to chart your life in this pattern. It works very well in many ways. The Hebrew calendar is based on this cycle. The weekly Torah portions keep it in constant action on our planet.

Native Americans look at cycles in an interesting manner. Imagine a circle. When you break out of the circle, you must complete the entire circumference before reentering at the same place.

The practice of vaulting is enhanced by recognizing cycles. You can connect to previous times to recognize your patterns as well as connect to previous circumstances.

Time is a tool for us to master in any number of ways. It exists, whether or not we make use of the knowledge. The warning in the Torah about astrologers refers to pagan astrologers, who skew Jewish timing. For other people on our planet, the passages are not against astrology and other teachings but rather a caution to be wary of the astrologer.

Jews are also advised in the Bible not to prognosticate, to do fortune-telling. I think that is good advice. A good process results when you really stop and listen. Carefully pay attention to all the patterns and information coming together in your life.

God has created an infinite number of patterns and cycles. Apparently, God never creates anything without reason, harmony, and connections. There is a reason for everything. It is always positive.

It is humans who make the errors in understanding and judgment. We have the choice to use time as a tool or not—just as we have the choice to utilize every other tool we have in our knowledge without limits. The qualifier is always to recognize the teacher or not. That is the case in all professions.

In astronomy, there is an optical illusion called retrograde motion. It is the result of planets and other phenomena having orbits that are circular or elliptical with different speeds.

In everyday observances on our planet itself, I observed this regularly when leaving Grand Central Station in New York City. Trains on adjacent tracks would appear as though they were moving backward. Without question, both trains were moving forward simultaneously. The appearance was quite the opposite.

Astrologers follow retrograde motion carefully, and there is, without question, a dramatic shift in energy related to various astronomical cycles and timing.

While it is not difficult to recognize retrograde motion in nearby planets, particularly Mercury, it is far more complicated in our times when we are entering the Aquarian from the Piscean Age.

It is quite possible there was an entry from Pisces into Aquarius in the 1960s. There was a remarkably appropriate song from the musical *Hair*,

"The Dawning of the Age of Aquarius." The words to describe Aquarius are quite appropriate.

The significant global events included the Second Vatican Council, the onset of the war in Vietnam, the Cuban Missile Crisis, and the assassination of President Kennedy followed by the assassinations of Robert Kennedy and Dr. Martin Luther King, Jr.

In accordance with the theory that we are now in the Age of Aquarius, there is the concept that the 1960s and the aforementioned events were in a period where the ages moved into Aquarius for a short time and then retrograded back into Pisces. We are now in the full two-thousand-year cycle of Aquarius.

21

SELAH: THE FIRST RELIGIOUS CONTROVERSY IN AMERICA

In 1635, the Antinomian Controversy began in Boston, just fifteen years after the Pilgrims arrived. Importantly, it was only five years after the Puritans arrived. The Winthrop Fleet began in 1630 and was composed of nonseparatists. The two groups were not alike in many ways, particularly in religious concepts. The Pilgrims, the separatists, living on the South Shore of Boston and on Cape Cod did not get into this heated argument. They were a separate society.

The Antinomian Controversy began with the division within the Church of England, the nonseparatists. The fight was about whether one could receive the Covenant of Grace solely by one's beliefs or whether one had to follow the Covenant of Works and do acts of kindness.

Whether they recognized it or not, this actually was a battle as to God being a verb or not. Were verbs, which are actions, decisive in our relationship with God? God said to Moses, "Know me by my deeds." This is the foundation of this book. Likewise, we are known to God by our deeds.

Appropriately, my ancestors were involved directly in this upheaval. While the movement was started by Reverend John Cotton of the First Church of Boston, ultimately, the main leaders were Anne Hutchinson and Reverend John Wheelwright, her husband's brother-in-law.

Hutchinson and Wheelwright were connected by marriages as well as beliefs. He spoke at the Fast Day in 1637, which was intended to restore unity. He intensified the battle exponentially.

There was a trial after the Fast Day speech by Wheelwright. Hutchinson and Wheelwright were banished. The Covenant of Grace was too radical for the traditionalists.

In the end, Hutchinson went to Rhode Island, and Wheelwright went to Exeter, New Hampshire, which was still bound to Massachusetts. It developed the Native Americans had already sold the land in Exeter to others. Wheelwright claimed a deed from 1629, which was impossible. The Winthrop Fleet came in 1630. Prior to 1630, the settlers were all in the Plymouth area and the cape. Settlers connected to the *Mayflower* passengers continued to trickle in, most settling in Boston and the North Shore; they were still connected to the Church of England.

Wheelwright's primary financial supporter had been Isaac Gross, owner of the Three Mariners, the second tavern in Boston. He became disenchanted with Wheelwright and left because of the false deed claim.

The Gross/LeGros family owned a major shipping company with powerful connections to the crown. They owned ships and taverns in the ports and market towns. His cousins actually owned the *Mayflower*. Isaac began their stake in taverns in the colonies. This put them in the network of word-of-mouth news as well as the forthcoming newspapers.

The effect on Isaac's family had already taken its toll. The Three Mariners had been taken over by his brother and sons. Isaac spent the rest of his life making real estate deals in the North Shore and Maine. Isaac had three sons and a daughter. The major chasm happened with his daughter, probably because of her choice of husband.

Isaac's four children had gone to the school in St. Petroc's in Bodmin, Cornwall, where they were born. The school was founded by Queen Elizabeth I and was attended by both boys and girls.

Isaac's eldest son married into the family of Samuel Cole, who owned the first tavern in Boston. He was one of many who rejected the Covenant of Grace when it became politically unpopular. Oddly, Cole ended up with history accounts asserting he owned the Three Mariners. Longfellow even wrote about it.

Isaac's youngest son followed into that sector of society as well.

The impact was permanent with Isaac's daughter Mary. He disowned her. It was undoubtedly intensified by the fact his children's mother had died in Cornwall. They migrated with his second wife, Katherine, their stepmother, who may have been illiterate.

I have published a book, *Good and Heavenly Counsel*, written by Grace Smith, who died in 1710 at the age of ninety-six. When she was dying, her minister, Reverend Samuel Treat, was shown her writings, and he had them published. Grace has not been identified other than as the wife of Ralph Smith. Historians have made absurd assertions as to her identity. My research indicates she was the daughter of Isaac Gross.

It was a thought when I was doing her genealogy that gave me the insight. Her grandson married a Gross. I had a "grok" about Ralph Smith, who became her husband in 1638. *Grok* means to understand profoundly through intuition or empathy. I had been transcribing her work for months, so her words and thoughts were in my mind. The flash of inspiration was Ralph saying, "You are not Mary Gross. You are my Mary Grace." Aha! It was just after she was disowned by her father. The name fit. Ultimately, she was just known as Grace. All the details and records fit.

Grace might have readily met Ralph Smith at the Three Mariners. He was one of the three teenagers who did the labor building Hingham, Massachusetts. He was quite enterprising. They married and had six children. Grace's brother, Clement, moved to Hingham and opened his own tavern. Grace's and Clement's families were intertwined significantly for generations.

Ralph and Grace moved to the cape. Ralph and his son, Samuel, were able to use the Gross family connections to have land for their tavern on the eastern end of the Cape, near Wellfleet. Through Grace's brother, Clement, and the Gross connections, Ralph was able to get a deed directly from the king of England. Great Island, the site, is on the National Register of Historic Places.

It was an amazing establishment with absolute privacy for whalers, pirates, and fishing. It was a well-appointed tavern with separate rooms for the elite and the hoi polloi, the commoners. Even the local natives came. Whales could be butchered in the basement, and there was a brothel upstairs.

The point of this chapter is that Grace's poetry and selection of verses fit the controversy precisely. She was brilliant, pious, educated, and kind. Her record is a remarkable alignment with the Covenant of Works. It shows the thoughts of a woman in that controversy who was dedicated to deeds. She had her strong, abiding faith, but she showed the basis of good and kind acts and deeds in her life.

I am a tenth-generation progeny of Grace Smith. I would be thrilled to discuss *God Is a Verb* with her. She never had that thought, but we would have great fun talking about the context. Considering God as a verb puts actions first. It is both God's actions as well as our own that predominate.

The ultimate test of our spiritual path and whether one thinks of God as a verb is whether you are dedicated to the golden rule as a continual demonstration of your relationship and your return to God.

Finally, remember that before many Days are out, a Holy, Just, and Impartial GOD, will call you to an Account, and Summons you before His Righteous Tribunal to answer for all the Mercies You ever Enjoyed, as Life, Health, Strengths, Sabbaths, Sermons, Chastisements. Yea, for all your Thoughts, Words and Actions. Therefore go Live and Work as that You may be able to Stand before the Son of Man in the Great Day of His Appealing, and Your Works abide the Trial; then you enter into your Lord and Master's Joy!

Mrs. Grace Smith

Eastham 1710

22

SELAH: SOULS

Our souls are in the image of God. Our bodies are not. It is actually hard to comprehend God having a form. God is without boundaries and limits. This is the reason our souls need a container, a place where they can exist in our bodies.

Selah—the soul of every living being is in the hands of God.

Our souls are totally aligned to the attributes of God. We are taught that souls were created before the acts of creating the physical components of the universe. They are eternal.

Selah—every act of human kindness strengthens
the spirit and illuminates the soul.

According to Rabbi Isaac Luria, souls can be divided and joined. The reasons God combines and separates souls all relate to the ultimate time when all of our souls can unite as one. Souls were created as one and then divided. Ultimately, they will join after the process of returning to God in awe, appreciation, and kindness. It is our job to care for the well-being of our souls and those particularly in our own family, our soul group.

At conception, a sperm and an egg are joined. The process of life has begun. This pair, a sperm and an egg, are compatible, not opposites. They are the basic pair in human existence. As soon as they are joined, a body begins to form. It is the house for the soul. It literally is a noun in every way.

Around the seventh month, a new stage is reached. The brain is formed. The two hemispheres are a pair. They are separated by a space. It is the only place in the body that is, literally, a space.

Our brains have two hemispheres. During the second trimester, the pair is formed: the right and left hemispheres of the brain. In the space between the pair is the space for the soul, the breath of life.

This is the applicable verse from Genesis: "Then God formed man of the dust of the ground, and breathed into his nostrils the breath of life; and man became a living soul" (Genesis 2:7).

We know that nostrils had to be fully formed and that there had to be a space for the soul. "And the Lord God formed man of dust from the ground, and He breathed into his nostrils the soul of life, and man became a living soul" (Genesis 2:7).

The soul is a verb. It literally is in the image of God, who is not corporal. It fills the space between the hemispheres of the brain, with our individual soul.

God breathes from Himself the breath of life, through the nostrils of the fetus into the space between the hemispheres of the brain, the space between our eyes. This space, which contains our soul, is regularly referred to as our third eye. At that point, the fetus becomes a human being containing the vital component, a soul.

> Our Soul
>
> God breathes our Soul, the breath of life, through our nostrils into the space between the hemispheres of our brain. It is often called our third eye.

Selah—our soul

Many mothers know precisely when that magical time happens. Suddenly, the baby has a soul, and the soul adapts to the life it will have in this lifetime. The last trimester is the time for the body to mature and the soul to begin the journey in this life.

When studying patterns, a clear position emerges. The day ninety degrees before your birthday is very important. It may well be possible that is the position wherein the body is developed to the point wherein the soul can be housed in the space between the hemispheres in our brains. This is an observation, and it may never be useful to others. The three trimesters before birth have a cyclical timing.

It has been noted that in preemies, when this period is short, the soul is, quite often, that which is described as an "old soul." They have been observed to have a very high level of consciousness.

It has also been noted that babies who will be adopted have a different journey in utero. They are often known to be connected to the family they will have, not the family who created the body, the house for the soul. The decisions regarding adoption may be made by both families around the time of the third trimester. The breath of life may show the relationship.

Selah.
You don't have a soul. You are a Soul. You have a body.
—C. S. Lewis

Our souls are absolutely in the image of God.
Our souls are verbs.
Our body is physical.
It is the house for our soul.
Our soul is our breath of life.
Our soul is a verb.

23

SELAH: EGO

There is an aspect of human behavior that is regularly outside of any pair and does not reflect back to God.

Ego is your consciousness of your own identity. It is also defined as oneself, especially as distinct from the world and other selves.

God does not have an ego. An ego is a human aspect and is not an attribute of God. It may be considered the human characteristic most separated from God.

Our souls are in the image of God and do not have ego.

> And God said, "Let us make man in our image, after our likeness, and they shall rule over the fish of the sea and over the fowl of the heaven and over the animals and over all the earth and over all the creeping things that creep upon the earth."
>
> And God created man in His image; in the image of God He created him; male and female He created them. (Genesis 1:26–27)

> This is the narrative of the generations of man; on the day that God created man, in the likeness of God He created him. (Genesis 5:1)

It is critical to comprehend God as a verb, an action, beingness. Our souls are in the image of God as an entity without dimensions.

One has to comprehend that God is formless and has no corporality in any manner.

Considering an image as requiring form is the limitation. Images may be only in the mind and may be entirely a perception or awareness. It is distinctly possible that an image may be a verb.

God does not have an ego. Egos are a function of our personal brains. Our souls and our brains are quite dissimilar. It is perhaps easiest to understand that our brains have a human function and are nouns. Our brains are part of our bodies. Our souls are not part of our bodies. They are a nonphysical entity contained in our bodies.

Our brains are nouns. Our souls are verbs. Our breath of life, our soul, enters when the body has developed sufficiently to contain our soul.

They are the most dissimilar pairing. They are not opposite but rather the penultimate challenge for every human bring to bring into harmony and equilibrium. Key to understanding the entire challenge is to recognize that God does not have an ego. Our souls do not have an ego. They are in the likeness of God and, therefore, have the same components and an alignment in the eternal cycle of creation and gratitude.

We must work to keep our own ego in balance. There is not one aspect of God that is commensurate with our egos. God has no ego.

All humans beings have both an ego and a soul. Egos are a clear and certain aspect of ourselves. We all need self-worth. Egos are not bad unless we make them dysfunctional and unbalanced. Having a healthy, balanced ego is the challenge for every person.

Our soul and our ego should work in the aspect of a pair, but when they do not, most decidedly, they function as incompatible, as opposites.

Rabbi Israel Heller has been my guide in this respect for many years. I respect this teaching very much and have never found an unworkable situation that was not ego centered or ego generated.

Our very equilibrium depends on how well we have balance in our own ego. It is our ego that establishes our separation from our soul itself as well as from other humans and God.

There are some teachings that are entirely egocentric. It is quite probable that God does not even deal with egocentric issues. God does not have an ego, so this is a trait that is outside His realm. I have experienced teachings that deny data. They do affirmations or prayers strictly formatted, and they tell God what to do. That is a mental manipulation. A truism is that "affirmations based on ego are mental manipulations." To be graphic, one could say, "Affirmations based on ego are mental masturbations." It is not healthy for our minds.

More than anything, these folks reject compassion. They will never resolve an issue because they love their mental gymnastics.

They are taught they are superior. That actually happens a lot with psychological venues. They are taught their teaching is the only way.

They are wrong.

A common, very common, characteristic in ego-dominant teachings and people is that they refuse to resolve any issue. It is never their fault. Realistically, it is always their fault. It is a perfect hierarchical mind-set. To deny resolution is an absolute violation of our challenge as humans to return to God in awe, appreciation, and compassion for all beings.

It can be said that our ego is the location for our free will. It is the absence of God. Our souls are directly connected and aligned to God. This is the ultimate challenge. Bring your ego into harmony with your soul.

There is a truism "Any computation based on insufficient data is always faulty." Egocentrism is invariably filled with insufficient and faulty data. It is a barrier to truth. An out-of-balance ego denies the rights of others and keeps only the priority of self.

A common teaching, which is entirely based on ego, is to turn the other cheek. It is not taught consistently with other Torah teachings. When anyone blocks resolution for another person, it is an act of extreme ego and cruelty. It only serves the ego of the doer, whether or not he or she feels entitled. It also works when not accepting apologies. It is a supreme control characteristic. The ego person is in control of the other person or persons. One group of ministers refuses data. They just get into their canned affirmations. They never have understanding or compassion. In the end, they are the losers. There is every probability that we face incompletions and denial of resolution when we go through the truth process at the end of life. The denial of resolution is an ugly action in every way.

These same people are fond of saying, "There are two sides to everything." That does not mean they are both right. It takes sufficient high-quality experience and wisdom to ascertain truth and justice. Disregarding facts and compassion are a clear and certain separation from God and God's reason for creating us. Where there is division, the best solution is a willingness to forge a common understanding. The more data, experience, introspection, and awareness one has, the more possible it is to create balance.

A clue to the depth of separation into ego is how judgmental a person is. A clue toward resolution is to keep working until you get to the truth. At least you will have attempted resolution. Truth does not have sides. Truth is.

Our souls and our egos are as close to opposite as possible. In fact, one could consider our egos as nouns and our souls as verbs.

It is interesting that God does not have a corporality or boundaries or an ego. God is a verb and our souls are verbs. Our souls are in the image of God. Our egos may be the ultimate separation from God.

Putting those two aspects of our being into harmony may be the ultimate challenge in our lives. Of course, we all need healthy egos.

The problem is having an egocentric context that is way out of balance. It happens far too often. Are ego issues the test when we go through the truth process at the termination of our lives? Are our egos our legacy to our families? Is sociopathic behavior essentially an ego problem?

Interestingly, the first, primary, and essential attribute on the tree of knowledge for the Way of Return is awareness—that awareness of self and others. Ego is the absolutely clear dominant factor in a failure to live with awareness.

A number of years ago, there was a craze for teaching "Looking out for number one." They certainly were not thinking about God, who is number One, capitalized. Egos are a function of our mind. They should be considered nouns. They are not connected to our souls, verbs. Humility is a valuable asset when connecting to God. Humility may be the most appropriate attribute when attempting to pair our egos to our souls.

Reflecting on one's soul is the obvious method to get order over ego.

The objective on the Way of Return is to have clarity. Ego may very well prevent clarity with other Torah teachings.

God is a verb. He does not have an ego. Our souls are verbs. Our souls have no ego. Our body, a noun, the house for our soul, has a component called ego. Egos are apparently found only in human beings. Egos are the major deterrent in our relationships with others. They are the primary obstacle in every aspect of the tree of knowledge.

Opinion is really the lowest form of human knowledge. It
requires no accountability, no understanding. The highest
form of knowledge … is empathy, for it requires us to suspend
our egos and live in another's world. It requires profound
purpose larger than the self kind of understanding.

—Bill Bullard

Ego is the absolute opposite of compassion. Our egos have no paired
aspect with anything else. Humans create and develop their own egos. Egos
are part of our freewill choice to create. God does not create opposites.
God creates pairs.

Humans have egos.
God does not.

24

SELAH: THE GOLDEN RULE

It is not complicated.

There is one rule: Be nice!
There is one question: Is it nice?
In other words, if it isn't nice, don't do it.

That is the basic principle of relatedness and the six-thousand-year challenge for humans on our planet.

Remarkably, over our planet, the major religions, as well as ethical and spiritual endeavors, all have a similar version of this maxim or rule. It is a component of a preponderance of organization and business charters and statements. It is called the ethic or law of reciprocity. A fine discussion and list can be found on *Wikipedia.* There are many extensive lists on the Internet.

It does not refer to or require a god. There is no specific religion. This teaching is found globally and is a guidepost for ethical atheists and agnostics as well as all manner of believers in God.

This maxim with dedication to action, rather than any belief, is my central concept that "God is a verb."

The first reference in the Torah is given in Leviticus.

Leviticus 19:18 says, "Thou shalt not take vengeance, nor bear any grudge against the children of thy people, but thou shalt love thy neighbor as thyself: I am the Lord."

Rabbi Hillel, who lived from 110 BC to 10 CE, taught "That which is hateful to you, do not do to your fellow. That is the whole Torah; the rest is the explanation; go and learn."

Jesus, who studied at Beit Hillel when Hillel was still alive, taught the paired aspect. It is found three times in the New Testament.

Matthew 7:12 says, "So whatever you wish that others would do to you, do also to them, for this is the Law and the Prophets."

And Luke 6:31 reads, "Do to others as you would have them do to you."

In 1948, the United Nations passed the Universal Declaration of Human Rights (UDHR).

> Now, Therefore THE GENERAL ASSEMBLY proclaims THIS UNIVERSAL DECLARATION OF HUMAN RIGHTS as a common standard of achievement for all peoples and all nations, to the end that every individual and every organ of society, keeping this Declaration constantly in mind, shall strive by teaching and education to promote respect for these rights and freedoms and by progressive measures, national and international, to secure their universal and effective recognition and observance, both among the peoples of Member States themselves and among the peoples of territories under their jurisdiction.

In 2008, Karen Armstrong's Charter for Compassion was introduced globally. The concluding statement follows.

> We urgently need to make compassion a clear, luminous and dynamic force in our polarized world. Rooted in a principled determination to transcend selfishness, compassion can break down political, dogmatic, ideological and religious boundaries. Born of our deep interdependence, compassion is essential to human relationships and to a fulfilled humanity. It is the path to enlightenment, and indispensable to the creation of a just economy and a peaceful global community.

Both are important in order to bring peace on this planet.

It is important to recognize we are on the cusp of the Age of Aquarius. We may have entered this age during the 1960s for a short period and then reversed back into the Piscean Age. It was the dawning of the Age of Aquarius.

When observing time in astronomy, there is an optical relationship wherein periods and aspects reverse, called retrograde, into the preceding cycle. Since cycles are elliptical, it is possible to see this phenomenon on our planet. I have observed this myself leaving Grand Central Station in New York City on a train. Because of the differences in speed, the other train appears to be in reverse, yet both are going forward.

Christianity and Islam are both Piscean Age religions. They reflect this mind-set. The two fish going in opposite directions show the dedication for opposites, which are hierarchical, rather than pairs. It is now a glorious time to readjust to the basic concept of the Age of Aquarius, the universal brotherhood of humankind.

The concept I am explaining as vaulting is very important. We are in the process of entry into Aquarius. The organizing principle is to be able to connect back in time and thought before the Piscean Age in order to shift into the Aquarian mind-set cleanly.

The Constitution of the United States is framed on the pattern of the tree of life. Our incredible constitution has the in-built capability to adapt and incorporate change. The patterns, both Jewish and Iroquoian, fit the changes. Our founding fathers did not want European concepts in our system of government. Our constitution is incredibly well designed to enable a healthy progress into the forthcoming period based on brotherhood. Our constitution is not flawed. It enabled a well-considered union that could adapt.

The phenomenal upheaval at the onset of the Piscean Age seems to be repeating as we enter Aquarius. I hope we can make the changes that are mandated.

If it isn't nice, don't do it.

25

SELAH: THE FOUR RS
OF RELATEDNESS

As humans, we seem to have an inordinate number of unresolved issues. Endings are left in the realm of our egos. Very often, things are terminated in our own point of view. It is simply debris that litters our lives.

The truth is self-awareness is the first step in relatedness. Apparently, upon studying the patterns in Taurus, one can see our lives are measured by our capacity and actions regarding others. Given our calendar, we are to measure time each week by having a day of jubilee with each other. When people have near-death experiences, very often, they tell of the truth process as one enters the transition stage. It is a flash sequence of one's soul journey featuring how one treated others.

"The evil eye" might well be called "the ego eye." Does it block your "third eye," that of your soul between your eyes? When you think about it, the evil eye is given in judgment, many times without even firsthand data. It is totally outside the tree of knowledge, outside of experience, and outside anyone's relationship with God. It is used as a final judgment and is never, ever appropriate or warranted.

This chapter is aimed at a few characteristics to hold as commonplace. They are being

- responsible—able to answer for one's conduct and obligations: *trustworthy*
- respectful—to show regard or consideration for

- responsive—the quality of being responsive, reacting quickly; as a quality of people, it involves appropriately responding with emotion and empathy to people and events (Handle matters, the sooner, the better. The longer the issue is not addressed, the larger and deeper it goes.)
- resolved—having the state of being resolved, cleared up, settled; as a verb, progressing from dissonance to consonance (Resolvancy is the desired objective.)

In the course of my learning, I was taught the importance of vows. When entering into a serious agreement, it is important to make a vow, a formal action of your own design and creation to formalize the pledge. It is mandatory when terminating a vow to make a similar dedicated formal vow. Otherwise, it is still in effect but without boundaries.

Take your vows seriously and respect them at all times. Otherwise, make certain they are resolved or completed.

26

THE LINWOOD EXPERIENCE

Linwood Spiritual Center is on an extraordinary site in Rhinebeck, New York, with a view straight down the Hudson River. When it was given to the Sisters of St. Ursula back in the 1960s, they first used it as a nursery and kindergarten for local children.

My doctor said, "My children come home every day singing happy songs." I enrolled my son immediately for the fall class. The children, their mothers, and the sisters were truly an idyllic group.

One of my favorite visions was watching the entire group with the sisters in their habits as they ascended a hill so the children could meet cows. It was a happy time for all.

Yes. They did come home singing. One of the activities was learning to count and sing in French as well as English. They knew the meaning of the songs. Great good fun!

Years later, when my son was entering college, I visited Mother Mary Francis, the head of the order. She was eighty-nine years old at the time. Instantly, she said, "Ah! Lance! I remember him well!" She went on to tell me stories about him playing with Scott, Andrew, Christopher, and others. She told me the games and activities Lancer liked best with each of them. Amazing upon amazing!

She also remembered my daughter, Lael, who came two years later. Lael especially loved her classmates Elizabeth and Bentley. Indeed!

One day in kindergarten, Lancer asked me to buy a whole bunch of big balloons. "Mother Mary Francis told us we could find God wherever there is air. I want God to have a place in my room!"

27

REMEMBER TO REMEMBER

God is a verb.

God is truth in action.

God is love in action.

Humans are nouns containing their souls, which are verbs. Our bodies are our house for our soul. Our image of God is our soul. Our egos are the absence of God. We must learn to manage our egos in order to fulfill our purpose as human beings on planet Earth. We were created and designed to relate to each other with compassion and joy.

Printed in the United States
By Bookmasters